EUROPE/AMERICA
1

NUCLEAR WEAPONS IN EUROPE

Andrew J. Pierre, Editor

William G. Hyland
Lawrence D. Freedman
Paul C. Warnke
Karsten D. Voigt

A Council on Foreign Relations Book

Published by
New York University Press
New York and London
1984

COUNCIL ON FOREIGN RELATIONS BOOKS

The Council on Foreign Relations, Inc., is a nonprofit and nonpartisan organization devoted to promoting improved understanding of international affairs through the free exchange of ideas. The Council does not take any position on questions of foreign policy and has no affiliation with, and receives no funding from, the United States government.

From time to time, books and monographs written by members of the Council's research staff or visiting fellows, or commissioned by the Council, or written by an independent author with critical review contributed by a Council study or working group are published with the designation "Council on Foreign Relations Book." Any book or monograph bearing that designation is, in the judgment of the Committee on Studies of the Council's board of directors, a responsible treatment of a significant international topic worthy of presentation to the public. All statements of fact and expressions of opinion contained in Council books are, however, the sole responsibility of the author.

First published in hard cover by New York University Press, Washington Square, New York, N.Y. 10003

Library of Congress Cataloging in Publication Data
Main Entry under title:

  Nuclear weapons in Europe.

  (Europe/America ; 1)
    1. Europe—Defenses—Addresses, essays, lectures.
2. Atomic weapons—Addresses, essays, lectures.
3. North Atlantic Treaty Organization—Addresses,
essays, lectures. I. Pierre, Andrew J. II. Hyland,
William, 1929-   . III. Council on Foreign Relations.
IV. Series.
UA646.N79 1983   355'.03304   83-26171
ISBN 0-8147-6590-4

The Project on
European-American Relations

Relations between Western Europe and the United States have become more turbulent in recent years. Divergences in interests and perceptions have grown. Many are questioning the fundamental assumptions of the postwar period. There is a broad consensus that the European-American relationship is in a state of transition.

A new generation is emerging and a number of social and cultural changes are under way that are also contributing to this transition. While our common heritage and values set limits on how far we may drift apart, there is an increasing recognition of the divergences between the United States and Europe on such critical issues as defense and arms control, policy toward the Soviet Union, East-West trade and technology transfer, West-West economic relations, North-South issues, and problems outside the NATO area. The challenge for statesmen will be to manage the differences—and where possible create a new Western consensus—in such a way as to enable the Alliance to adapt to new circumstances while preserving its basic character.

The relatively simple world of the postwar period is gone. Americans today appear to have less understanding of European perspectives and Europeans less appreciation of American views. There is much handwringing about the trans-Atlantic malaise, but less constructive thinking about how to manage and, where possible, reduce our differences.

The project is designed to identify and clarify the differences in interests and perspectives affecting critical issues in the European-American relationship, thereby enhancing understanding across the Atlantic. Approximately three issues per year will be selected for examination on a rolling basis over the next three years. The issues will be those that are most likely to create friction in the period ahead.

A short book will be published on each issue. European and American authors with points of view that differ from each other but represent important strands of thought in their respective societies will contribute analyses of the problem and offer their policy prescriptions. We hope that by disaggregating the issues in this manner, we can make a constructive contribution to the Atlantic debate.

An advisory group of Council members, with the participation of European guests, will help choose the issues and will discuss the ideas in the manuscripts prior to publication. They are, however, in no way responsible for the conclusions, which are solely those of the authors.

This is the first book in the series. The next book will address the impact of unemployment on trade and protectionism, economic growth, and the politics of European-American economic relations.

We would like to thank the Rockefeller Foundation, the Andrew W. Mellon Foundation and the German Marshall Fund for their assistance in supporting this project.

Cyrus R. Vance

The editor would like to thank Winston Lord, Paul Kreisberg, Pat Bridges, Grace Darling, Norman Jacobs, David Kellogg, Kay King, and Robert Valkenier for their assistance in the production of this book.

The Project on European-American Relations is under the auspices of the Council's Studies Program.

Contents

About the Authors

Lawrence D. Freedman is Professor of War Studies at King's College, University of London. Previously he was Head of Policy Studies at the Royal Institute for International Affairs (Chatham House); Research Associate at the International Institute for Strategic Studies; and a Research Fellow of Nuffield College, Oxford. He is the author of *The Evolution of Nuclear Strategy, Britain and Nuclear Weapons, U.S. Intelligence and the Soviet Strategic Threat* and other works.

William G. Hyland is a Senior Associate at the Carnegie Endowment for International Peace and Editor-elect of *Foreign Affairs*. From 1977 to 1981 he was a Senior Fellow, as well as an Associate in the office of Henry A. Kissinger, at the Georgetown Center for Strategic and International Studies. He served as Deputy Assistant to the President for National Security Affairs from 1975 to 1977 and as Director of the Bureau of Intelligence and Research in the Department of State from 1973 to 1975. In addition, Mr. Hyland was a member of the National Security Council Staff from 1969 to 1973 and an analyst with the Central Intelligence Agency from 1954 to 1969.

Karsten D. Voigt is a member of the Bundestag. He was elected in 1976 and is currently the Social Democratic Party leader in the Foreign Affairs Committee. Since 1981 he has been one of the Foreign and Defense Policy spokesmen for the SPD. Formerly, Mr. Voigt was Vice President of the International Union of Socialist Youth from 1973 to 1975 and National Chairman of the Young Socialists from 1969 to 1972. He is the author of *Paths Toward Disarmament* and numerous articles on foreign and defense policy.

Paul C. Warnke is a partner in the law firm of Clifford and Warnke. He served as Director of the Arms Control and Disarmament Agency and as chief U.S. negotiator at the Strategic Arms Limitation Talks from 1977 to 1978. In addition, Mr. Warnke was Assistant Secretary of Defense for International Security Affairs from

1967 to 1969 and General Counsel at the Department of Defense in 1966-67.

Andrew J. Pierre is a Senior Fellow at the Council on Foreign Relations and the Director of the Project on European-American Relations. Formerly on the staff of the Brookings Institution and the Hudson Institute, he has also taught at Columbia University and served with the Department of State as a Foreign Service Officer in Washington and abroad. Mr. Pierre is the author of *The Global Politics of Arms Sales, Nuclear Politics: The British Experience with an Independent Strategic Force, Nuclear Proliferation: A Strategy for Control* and other works.

Andrew J. Pierre

Introduction

The role of American nuclear weapons in the defense of Western Europe has been a subject of debate almost since the inception of the NATO Alliance itself. After all, what is at issue is the fundamental link between Western Europe's security and that of the United States, and therefore the credibility of the American nuclear guarantee. Charles de Gaulle sharply challenged America's reliability as a nuclear protector in the late 1950s, and the debate over the multilateral nuclear force in the early 1960s revealed many of the difficulties of managing the Alliance's nuclear affairs. During the past four years, however, a new height of controversy has been reached, and for some there is a deeper fear of war and a growing mistrust of the Alliance. These developments followed the NATO decision of December 1979 to deploy 572 U.S. intermediate-range nuclear missiles in Western Europe while at the same time undertaking arms control negotiations with the Soviet Union.

The deployments began in November 1983, but they are not scheduled to be completed until 1988. The Soviet Union, in response, walked away from the negotiations on intermediate-range nuclear forces (INFs) in Geneva saying that further participation in these talks while NATO was deploying its planned 464 ground-launched cruise missiles and 108 Pershing IIs would be an "impossibility." This was soon followed by the Soviet departure from both the strategic arms negotiations and the talks on mutual and balanced force reductions in Vienna which deal with conventional arms.

Clearly, we reached an important juncture at the end of 1983. Yet the issues are far from settled. In the short run we will need to see if Moscow makes good on its announced intention to put the United States in an "analogous position" through a series of countermeasures. It has said it might increase the seaborne threat to the United States by moving ballistic missile nuclear submarines closer to American shores, or by deploying new sea-to-land, long-range cruise missiles on surface ships or submarines. The placing of SS-20s on the Siberian peninsula, aimed at Alaska and the Northwest of the United States, is evidently under consideration. In Europe, the Soviets have indicated their intention to accelerate the deployment of new SS-21, SS-22 and SS-23 nuclear missiles in East Germany, Czechoslovakia and possibly elsewhere within the Warsaw Pact. In addition, Moscow could increase still further the number of SS-20s it has targeted on Western Europe since it abrogated the "moratorium" by which it claims to have been abiding since 1982. The West will have to carefully consider if and how it wants to respond to these steps. Meanwhile, the Alliance's ability to complete the full-scale deployment of the 572 missiles in five countries will be tested. (Belgium and the Netherlands have yet fully to agree to accept their share of the missiles.) At the same time, no doubt, pressures will develop for renewed negotiations on the INF issues in some forum.

The agenda for the longer run is still more important, however, for it involves fundamental questions which badly need to be re-examined by NATO governments and their concerned citizenry: Should the security of Western Europe continue indefinitely to depend upon the United States and, if so, to what degree and in what form? What role should American nuclear weapons based on the continent have in the defense of Western Europe, including its defense against a solely conventional attack? What should be the role of shorter range, battlefield nuclear weapons in NATO strategy? Can improvements in conventional weapons reduce the dependency upon nuclear arms, and to what extent? Should NATO adopt a declaratory policy of "no-first-use"? How can arms limitation on nuclear weapons in Europe be negotiated, and what type of forum would be most appropriate? Should the talks on intermediate-range systems be kept separate from the strategic arms reduction talks (START), as they have in recent years, or should they now be merged into a larger negotiation? Do the French and British forces need to be accounted for, and how could negotiations encompass them? Beyond this, what is the appropriate place of arms control in Western security policy and in the future evolution of East-West relations?

These are among the issues addressed in this volume. They will be the staple of the European-American discourse on nuclear strategy and arms control during the 1980s. Their emergence in the public debate during the past few years was the largely unintended (at least by NATO governments) result of the 1979 decision on the deployment of intermediate-range weapons. They are likely to be even more widely debated in the next few years on both sides of the Atlantic by a new generation that has only recently awakened to these issues and which clearly is not prepared to accept automatically the Atlantic orthodoxies of the postwar generation.

The four authors of this book present contrasting approaches to these questions. Although two are European and two are American, the dividing lines in their analyses are not solely, or even primarily, determined by geography or nationality but rather by political perspectives and interpretations. Each of them is a recognized expert, and three of the four have considerable governmental or political experience in dealing with these problems. All four agree on the need to think through the role of nuclear weapons in the defense of Western Europe in the broad geopolitical context of East-West relations. They seek in these pages to make a contribution to the necessary review of NATO strategy, force structure and arms control. Yet they differ considerably in their analyses and in their policy recommendations. This, in turn, reflects their differing assumptions about world politics and the requirements of nuclear deterrence.

Differing Assumptions

For William Hyland the basic issue is not the number or kind of American nuclear weapons to be stationed in Europe; nor are the Soviet missiles targeted upon Western Europe the heart of the matter. These are merely the "terrain" over which the contest is being waged. The fundamental issue is "the continuing struggle over the future of Europe: whether Western Europe will continue to seek its security through close dependence on the United States, or will gradually move toward a more autonomous position; whether the United States is capable of both reassuring its allies and sustaining a credible deterrent against the Soviet Union." He emphasizes the Soviet Union's political aims in Western Europe.

Karsten Voigt, on the other hand, stresses the dangers of war. "Anyone living, as do the Germans," he writes, "along the borders separating the NATO countries from the Warsaw Pact nations is aware that even a war waged solely with conventional weapons leaves few chances of survival. This is all the more true of a war fought with nuclear weapons—even if 'only' with so-called tactical nuclear weapons, of which thousands are stored in Europe. Their combat use would convert large parts of Europe into desert." Voigt puts the emphasis on reducing the nuclear component of NATO strategy, on the urgency of various types of arms control, and on the importance of replacing nuclear deterrence—which he views as overly risky—by an East-West "security partnership."

Lawrence Freedman's basic concern is the confusion that has arisen, even among stalwart supporters of NATO, regarding the rationale underlying the Alliance's nuclear policy. His contribution, therefore, reexamines the purposes for which NATO requires nuclear weapons in place in Europe, and proposes some changes in the structure of NATO's nuclear arsenal. Freedman, like Hyland, generally supports NATO's "dual-track decision."

Paul Warnke, like Voigt, is a skeptic. He believes that the "employment of nuclear weapons by NATO could under almost no conceivable circumstances contribute to a successful defense." He comes to this view with the conviction that no American president would retaliate against non-nuclear Soviet aggression by launching a nuclear first strike. It is no longer reasonable, Warnke argues, to base NATO nuclear strategy on the myth that he would.

Military and Political Rationales for INF

Whether or not there is a *military* need to deploy ground-launched cruise missiles and Pershing IIs is a key issue in the debate within the West. It is striking that only Freedman makes a strong case for such a military necessity. He points out that the 1979 deployment decision was not simply one of "modernizing" NATO's nuclear capability; it had the effect of an important shift in policy. When the Thor and Jupiter missiles, which were capable of reaching the

Soviet Union, were taken out of Western Europe in the early 1960s, it was not because of age, but the result of a deliberate political decision not to have missiles of such range based in Europe; presumably they could make escalation to the strategic level too rapid or easy. The INF deployments represent a reversal of that policy and are being made at the request of the Europeans who were concerned about the growth of Soviet nuclear capabilities targeted upon Western Europe; they go, he believes, against a long-standing American inclination to oppose the basing of inter-mediate-range weapons in Europe. Freedman does not base his support for the INF deployments on the often-cited need to "match" the SS-20 deployments. Rather, he believes that their physical presence on European soil will dispel any Soviet illusions about confining the consequences of a nuclear strike to Central or Western Europe. Thus, he contends, the new deployments will not only provide reassurance to the Europeans, but will significantly enhance deterrence and affect Soviet calculations by posing a genuine threat of escalation.

Warnke disagrees. The INF deployments cannot markedly improve existing deterrence. All important military, industrial and urban facilities in the Warsaw Pact's geographic area are already well covered by the 10,000 warheads now carried on American intercontinental and submarine-launched ballistic missiles and strategic bombers. If the Soviet Union should strike a European city or NATO base with an SS-20, he is confident that the United States would respond in kind with a Minuteman or Trident missile, or an air-launched cruise missile. Indeed, the notion that an American president would more readily launch a Pershing II from West Germany than a Minuteman III from the continental United States implies a belief that Soviet retaliation would be against the launching point—a very "decoupling" idea in itself. Warnke argues that there is no military need for 572 additional warheads to strike enemy targets. Their installation in West Germany in particular will reduce, rather than increase, European security. The reader, thus, is presented with two well-reasoned, but diametrically opposed, judgments regarding the military utility of the INF deployments.

All four authors underscore the *political* dimension. For Hyland the Euromissile debate is a critical test of the Alliance's will to resist and to defend itself. The changed strategic environment of the 1970s marked by the establishment of overall strategic parity between the United States and the U.S.S.R., the impending vulnerability of American intercontinental ballistic missiles (ICBMs) to a first strike, the continuing imbalance of conventional forces in Europe, and the growing imbalance in European theater nuclear forces created by the new SS-20s and Backfire bombers raised serious questions about the credibility of the U.S. guarantee to protect Europe. The purpose of strengthening theater nuclear capabilities was to reassure the allies that Europe's defense was coupled to that of the United States. (How needed this was is a matter of conjecture; Freedman suggests that there was more concern about declining credibility in the United States than in Europe.) The Soviets, Hyland argues, have sought to weaken ties between the United States and Europe, and especially between Washington and Bonn. The deployment of the SS-20s was part of an effort to change radically the balance and the European perception of that balance. Even if there were no agreed upon military doctrine to justify all of the deployments, especially the Pershing IIs (he observes that there was only a minimal relationship between the 572 number chosen in 1979 and such conventional military criteria as target coverage or survivability), once the public debate flared in Europe, the missile deployments came to be regarded as a test of Alliance solidarity.

Voigt is far less concerned that the Soviet Union might attempt to use its SS-20s and other nuclear weapons targeted upon Western Europe to blackmail the continent because, in his view, this would provoke a strong counter-response. Also, he does not believe that the Russians have shown any desire to expand militarily into Western Europe. The problem confronting Europe is less that of containing Soviet military expansion than of organizing lasting, peaceful coexistence in the face of continuing conflict between two adversarial political systems. Many Europeans fear that the two nuclear superpowers might think it possible to wage a limited and controlled nuclear war in Europe. Since he doubts such a possibility, Voigt suggests a reexamination of NATO's doctrine of flexible response with a view toward decreasing the number and the function of nuclear weapons in the the Alliance's strategy. In this context, the Pershing II deployments should be dropped, as the targets for which they are intended are already adequately covered.

Battlefield Nuclear Weapons

The debate in recent years over the new intermediate-range nuclear forces has, not surprisingly, raised many questions about the purpose and utility of the short-range battlefield or tactical nuclear weapons. These weapons, consisting of aerial bombs, artillery rounds, atomic land mines, short-range missiles, and air-defense missiles in and at sea around Europe totaled approximately 7,000 at the end of the 1970s. First placed in Europe in 1954 as a means of countering Soviet land forces, their usefulness has often been questioned. Although they may provide some significant steps in the ladder of escalation, their use could also wreak havoc on the defender's own territory. It is far from clear that their use could be limited successfully without leading to an all-out nuclear conflagration. An additional problem is that many battlefield nuclear weapons are located near the front lines, and if not utilized, could be overrun and captured thereby creating pressures to "use them or lose them."

All four authors reach the conclusion that NATO's battlefield nuclear weapons should be scaled down considerably in number. This process was started by a 1979 decision to reduce them by 1,000 and was furthered by a second decision reached on October 28, 1983, to withdraw another 1,400 warheads during the next several years. Many of the weapons to be taken out are obsolete, such as the land mines and the Nike-Hercules anti-aircraft missile, so it made sense to eliminate them irrespective of the INF deployments. Freedman points out that with the INF program under way, the United States has now adequately confirmed its commitment to the nuclear defense of Europe. He also notes that the maintenance of battlefield nuclear weapons diverts resources from the improvement of conventional forces. Taking these two factors into consideration, he recommends that battlefield weapons be dramatically reduced in number. The other authors appear to agree with Hyland in his observation that battlefield weapons have a waning military rationale and carry an increasingly high political price. But two of the authors suggest that some short-range weapons be modernized and located further from the front, yet still maintain the capability to attack second-echelon targets in Eastern Europe.

The majority sentiment is in favor of unilateral cuts rather than negotiated reductions. Unilateral cuts in battlefield nuclear weapons are simpler and are seen as providing a political argument against the anti-nuclear movement. This goes against the pattern of East-West arms control talks of past decades, however, and might become less attractive if the Soviets increase their short-range nuclear arsenals in Europe. NATO, moreover, has not obtained as much credit from the public as it might have for the unilateral reductions it has already made. Voigt states that for the Federal Republic of Germany a reduction in the new generation of Soviet short-range missiles is as desirable as a substantial reduction of SS-20s. He would negotiate further reductions in such weapons with the Soviet Union and associate the negotiations with the INF forum.

Conventional Defense

If the role of nuclear weapons in the defense of Europe is to be reduced, the corollary should be the strengthening of conventional forces. How, specifically, this might be done, and what the benefits and costs would be of revising the NATO force posture in this manner, are outside the principal focus of this book and may well be discussed in another volume in this series. Voigt nevertheless properly raises the question in suggesting the "conventionalization" of NATO strategy and in commenting that the current strategy of "flexible response," which was adopted by the Alliance in 1967, may not be adequate to the times. He would like to move away from relying upon the threat of the first-use of nuclear weapons by taking advantage of current improvements in conventional weapons technology.

In Hyland's view, on the other hand, there is a "near obsession" with strengthening conventional defense on the part of those in Europe and the United States who want to reduce reliance on nuclear weapons. Conventional defense is not a panacea for NATO's problems. Just as nuclear weapons are not a substitute for conventional forces, conventional forces cannot substitute for the deterrent function of nuclear weapons either. Western deterrence can never rest upon conventional forces alone, no matter how strong, because Soviet conventional forces are likely to remain stronger than NATO's in Central Europe, and because geography favors the U.S.S.R., thus requiring the forward defense of West Germany. Flexible response, in Hyland's view, cannot be replaced by a doctrine of conventional response and no-first-use of nuclear weapons without risking the long-term neutralization of West Germany. Freedman joins him in opposition to a declared policy of no-first-use of nuclear weapons, pointing out that no-*early*-first-use is already implicitly agreed upon in NATO's consultative and nuclear release procedures. He also would like to see more emphasis on the particular horrors, risks and uncertainties of conventional war. The deterrent value of conventional arms tends to be disregarded in the stress on the even greater evils of nuclear war.

Merger of INF and START

There is an interesting consensus among the authors that contrasts with the policy of the Reagan Administration regarding the next steps in developing arms control for intermediate-range nuclear forces in Europe. All favor a merging of the INF and START negotiations. In Warnke's opinion the intermediate-range nuclear forces can only be successfully negotiated in a bargaining forum in which all strategic weapons systems are available for discussion and for trade-offs. The separation of these negotiations, several of the authors remind us, was a historical accident created by the particular political circumstances of 1981 when the SALT II treaty was set aside, new strategic arms talks had not begun, and the implementation of the deployment part of the 1979 dual-track decision appeared to depend upon the existence of arms control negotiations. Freedman notes that the separation of the INF from the START negotiations has two disadvantages. First, it weakens the link between central strategic and intermediate-range nuclear forces and thus reduces the perception that ground-launched cruise missiles and Pershing IIs will contribute to escalation, thereby ensuring that deterrence does not fail. Second, it encourages comparison with Soviet forces of equivalent range (i.e., the SS-20s), while ignoring other nuclear forces targeted on Western Europe. With the beginning of the deployments, Hyland adds, a merger of the START and INF negotiations could be an attractive, face-saving compromise to avoid a complete breakdown in negotiations on intermediate-range forces.

The authors also favor taking the British and French nuclear forces into account in the negotiations. Several believe that the Soviets have a legitimate point in asking that European nuclear forces targeted on them be included, and that it is implausible to completely leave out such forces from all East-West nuclear negotiations. The merging of the INF and START negotiations would greatly facilitate the inclusion of the British and French nuclear weapons in the total count. It would, moreover, make them less of a problem because their relatively small numbers would be less significant in the context of global negotiations covering the entire American and Soviet strategic arsenals, than if they were handled in separate European negotiations. Freedman recommends direct bilateral deals between Moscow and London and Paris.

As Hyland describes them, the INF negotiations thus far have been "bizarre." He and Freedman are critical of the "zero option" put forth by the United States in 1981, not only because of its unnegotiability, but because it undermines the essential rationale of NATO's original 1979 decision. In their view some capability for reaching the Soviet Union from Europe is necessary for purposes of extended deterrence and the strategic coupling of the United States and Europe. The zero option not only was flawed in its strategic logic, but would have allowed the Soviets—as they deployed shorter range SS-21, SS-22 and SS-23 missiles—to achieve an imbalance in such tactical nuclear weapons.

The failure of Washington and Moscow to accept the formula worked out by Ambassador Paul Nitze and his counterpart Yuli Kvitsinsky, in their now famous "walk in the woods" in July 1982, is seen in varying degrees by most of the authors as an important lost opportunity. The warhead numbers involved, about 300 for each side (actually 75 SS-20 missiles for the Soviet Union with three warheads each, and 75 land-based cruise missile launchers of four missiles each for the United States) are seen as acceptable; so is the abandonment of the Pershing II deployments in return for

Soviet willingness to drop its insistence on compensation for the British and French forces.

Arms Control Proposals

Each of the authors presents some proposals regarding future arms control talks. If there are separate INF negotiations, Paul Warnke would have as a goal a return to the 600 to 700 warhead level on intermediate-range missiles that the Soviets had for many years prior to 1977. Anything that would approximately restore the status quo by scrapping the remaining SS-4s and SS-5s and destroying significant numbers of SS-20s should be acceptable to the West. A Soviet capability of 200 SS-20s, split equally between those aimed at Asian targets and those directed toward NATO Europe, would be a successful outcome. Under his preferred solution of folding INF weapons into a larger negotiation on strategic forces, Warnke would seek common ceilings subject to phased reductions. There would be overall limits on the total number of launchers and on nuclear warheads applicable to both intercontinental and intermediate-range forces. Thus the SS-20s would be lumped together with ICBMs, and they would be reduced in a phased manner. The effect of this, Warnke suggests, would be to reduce the targeting of Europe, as Soviet planners would be reluctant to use up a significant part of a dwindling entitlement on missiles that could not reach targets in the United States. Similarly, American planners would have to consider how large a portion of their weapons entitlement within the common ceiling they would want to allocate to weapons based in Western Europe that are less survivable and that may be less stabilizing than those of intercontinental range.

William Hyland argues that the Alliance's dual-track policy is basically sound and should be maintained. Accordingly, NATO must now proceed with a significant deployment of American nuclear missile forces in Europe. He would leave the Pershing II to future negotiating dynamics. The deployment of Pershing IIs is militarily desirable because of their hard-target capabilities and quick reaction time, but he would be willing to abandon them in return for significant Soviet concessions at the negotiating table. Hyland strongly cautions against stopping the deployments at what he calls a "token" level of (around 50) American missiles. This, he believes, would be a political and military debacle, the long-term consequences of which would return to haunt both the United States and the allies. With the breakdown in the negotiations, and the announced Soviet intention to initiate some counter-deployments, it is politically imperative that NATO maintain a solid front. A halt in the deployments at too low a level, Hyland believes, would leave the Soviet threat to Europe largely unaffected, would fail to firmly achieve recoupling, and would damage the credibility of the United States.

Lawrence Freedman's prescription is somewhat similar to that of Hyland. The placement of some intermediate-range forces in Europe is necessary for military reasons. But since the actual number of SS-20s does not matter enormously once a "certain level" of NATO deployments have been made, there should be no worry about accepting slightly larger Soviet numbers as long as the legitimacy of the NATO deployments has been accepted by the men in the Kremlin. If all that NATO has to "sweeten the pill" for the Soviets is the abandonment of the Pershing IIs, then he would be willing to put this forward in the negotiations since their strategic purposes can be adequately fulfilled by cruise missiles. On the other hand, warns Freedman, the United States cannot accept an outcome that leaves the threat to Japan and other states in the Far East unconstrained while the threat to Western Europe is limited.

Karsten Voigt proposes a formula which links the postponement of the NATO INF deployments to Soviet reductions of SS-20s in a succession of time periods. Specifically, for each month the placement of U.S. missiles in Europe is postponed, the Soviet Union would have to dismantle ten SS-20s. Since the Soviet Union has already indicated its willingness to reduce 90 of the 250 SS-20s aimed at Western Europe, this would provide a minimum of nine more months during which negotiations could proceed. The longer term aim is a negotiated compromise with such drastic reductions in SS-20 missiles that the new NATO deployments would be rendered superfluous. Voigt suggests that NATO review again whether the military purpose of intermediate-range forces could be taken over by sea-based systems, either through modernization of the submarines presently assigned to the Supreme Allied Commander in Europe, or by supplementing or replacing present capabilities with new sea-based systems. This was looked at in 1978-79 by the High Level Group of NATO, but he cites the development of weapons technology, and what he perceives to be the politically unconvincing case made earlier for not proceeding with sea-based systems, as reasons for a reexamination at this time. In addition, Voigt endorses the Palme Commission's proposal for a nuclear-weapons free zone extending approximately 150 kilometers in each direction from the border between NATO and the Warsaw Pact.

The commencement of the deployments will not end the debate over the role of nuclear weapons in the defense of Europe. Nor would any possible initial agreement in Geneva provide the resolution for all dimensions of the arms control problem in Europe. What is fundamentally involved is the whole question of Western policy toward the Soviet Union and the development of East-West relations.

It was perhaps unfortunate that the NATO dual-track decision of 1979—a decision seen by most at the time as basically intended to rectify a growing military imbalance created by the growth of Soviet nuclear power in Europe during the second half of the 1970s—became part of a wider debate as a consequence of Afghanistan, the non-ratification of SALT II, intra-Alliance divisions over such issues as economic sanctions, and the period of heightened East-West tensions during the early 1980s. Inevitably the INF deployments came to acquire a highly symbolic role: to some they were an instrument of confrontation and their envelopment in an arms control "solution" was seen as essential to avoiding nuclear war; to others they became a sine qua non in providing for Europe's security and in averting a political defeat of the West by the Soviet Union. The true importance of the deployments in the overall context of Western security may have been over-dramatized by all sides.

Nevertheless, Europe's nuclear dilemmas are now at the top of the agenda of the Western Alliance. How they are resolved, or managed, will have enormous consequences for both East-West relations and such intra-Alliance questions as the future of a divided Germany, the development of Western Europe as a political and, perhaps, defense entity, and the future relationship between the United States and Western Europe. On all these crucial issues there are important and very legitimate differences of views across the Atlantic and within the countries on both sides of the Atlantic. This volume is designed to explicate some of the different perspectives on nuclear weapons in Europe and thereby make a contribution to a more informed European-American debate.

December 1983

William G. Hyland

The Struggle for Europe: An American View

The current conflict between the United States and the Soviet Union is not really about the number or kinds of American nuclear weapons scheduled to be stationed in Europe. Even the Soviet missiles targeted against Western Europe are not the true heart of the matter. This is terrain over which the contest is being waged. The fundamental issue is the continuing struggle over the future of Europe: whether Western Europe will continue to seek its security through close dependence on the United States, or will gradually move toward a more autonomous position; whether the United States is capable of both reassuring its allies and sustaining a credible deterrent against the Soviet Union.

This phase of the struggle for Europe began in the mid-1970s. In a broad sense it is comparable to earlier phases, especially the conflict over West German rearmament in the early 1950s and the Sputnik crisis of 1957-58, and is reminiscent of the multilateral nuclear force (MLF) controversy of the 1960s. What distinguishes the present period is that it is unfolding in drastically altered strategic and political circumstances. In earlier East-West clashes the underlying reality of the nuclear dominance of the United States set an implicit limit to each Soviet thrust. That clear superiority has been replaced by a rough, global equilibrium, but, at the same time, a severe European imbalance in intermediate-range nuclear weapons has developed. In each preceding crisis, Western unity was never seriously at risk. Indeed, Western solidarity was the underlying reality girding American policy. Now, the maintenance of that very unity is severely tested by the East and seriously questioned on both sides of the Atlantic.

American policy thus has two immediate objectives: first, to restore a credible strategic and European defense posture that is not only persuasive to the Soviet Union, but also reassuring to Europe;

and second, to accomplish these ends while shoring up an increasingly fragile Western unity. In addition, and perhaps most difficult, the United States must achieve these aims without foreclosing the option of reestablishing a better relationship with the Soviet Union.

The Disintegration of Deterrence

As late as the fall of 1973, during the Middle East crisis, the United States could claim with some conviction that its nuclear predominance was still decisive in world affairs. A rare American nuclear alert brought a swift halt to a gathering crisis with the Soviet Union. But even then it was increasingly clear that American nuclear superiority was inexorably slipping away. As early as February 1969, during his first trip to Europe, President Richard Nixon warned the Western allies that the era of U.S. nuclear supremacy was ending. However, the full consequences of such a profound change in power relationships were obscured by the advent of détente. Moreover, the Europeans preferred not to contend with the unpalatable military alternatives, especially those that would have required a vast increase in defense efforts in the midst of an era of diminished tensions. Both the Americans and the Europeans were content with the highly ambiguous strategy of flexible response and the incomplete contingency plans for the actual first-use of nuclear weapons in Europe. A strong European preference was to limit any initial use of nuclear weapons by NATO to a "demonstration." This inability to agree on a serious policy signaled a breakdown in strategy and it allowed the persistence of the comforting illusion that deterrence was indefinitely credible, regardless of the balance of forces.

If Europe feigned indifference, the United States could not. On the contrary, for the past decade, the United States has had to make a major effort to cope with a new strategic environment distinguished by: (1) the establishment of an overall strategic parity between the United States and the U.S.S.R.; (2) the impending vulnerability of U.S. intercontinental ballistic missiles (ICBMs) to a first strike; (3) the continuing imbalance of conventional forces in Europe; and (4) the growing imbalance in European theater nuclear forces created by the deployments of the new Soviet SS-20 missile and the Backfire bomber.

The U.S. effort has been sporadic and, on certain issues, still-born. But judged as a whole, the United States has been modestly successful in adjusting its forces and its long-term strategy to the new era. It has been less successful in conducting this change in concert with its European allies. It has been least successful in integrating military changes with political and diplomatic efforts, including arms control. The consequence of this last is that the United States finds itself caught up in a major struggle with the U.S.S.R. that could seriously jeopardize much of the effort that has been accomplished since 1974, when then-Secretary of Defense James Schlesinger began to outline a new American strategy.

Strategic parity, of course, raised serious questions about the credibility of the U.S. guarantee to protect Europe by a strategy (flexible response) that ultimately rested on a threat of escalation to intercontinental weaponry. The doctrine was repeatedly reaffirmed by Washington and by the Alliance as a whole, but as American statesmen later confessed, these repeated assurances were not genuinely believed in American policymaking councils. Credibility was clearly waning by the time of the first SALT (Strategic Arms Limitation Treaty) agreements in 1972. By 1974 an effort was well under way to cope with the worst and most alarming aspects of the problem—namely, to repair the credibility of the highest level of escalation, the employment of strategic forces. Should the United States be forced to engage in nuclear escalation, American strategists believed that there had to be an option other than attacking the population and industrial centers of the Soviet Union: credibility could be restored most quickly through adjustments in targeting options. To provide "limited" responses, it was argued that the Soviet perception of U.S. strategy would be enhanced if the U.S. were in a position to order discrete retaliatory attacks, especially against selected Soviet military targets. Faced with the prospect of such a response, the Soviet Union would still be deterred.

This was a partial solution, eventually announced as the "Schlesinger doctrine" and officially incorporated in National Security Decision Memorandum 242. It was an essential step, for it

addressed the least credible components of the escalatory chain—
assured destruction of Soviet cities. But it was never intended to be
more than a stopgap. Its ultimate validity would be confirmed by
further steps including rebuilding conventional defense forces, refurbishing the nuclear arsenal stationed in Western Europe and, of
course, continuing the strategic modernization based on the B-1,
the Trident submarine, and the MX missile, while developing
cruise missiles.

The next step was the effort to move forward on conventional
defense under the Carter Administration in 1977-78. This was
welcomed in Europe and adopted by NATO as a long-term defense program. There was a momentary public panic produced by
leaks of Presidential Review Memorandum 10, which seemed to
contemplate giving up West German territory at the outset of a
European war. This gaffe was repaired by Presidential Directive 18
which restored the "forward defense" of West Germany. According to former National Security Advisor Zbigniew Brzezinski,
however, unnamed parties in the American internal debate at the
time proposed reducing U.S. troops in Europe. Despite this episode, small shifts in the U.S. deployment of ground troops from
southern to northern Germany, pledges of increased defense
spending, and a broad NATO program of force improvement reflected a new seriousness in conventional defense planning.

But American views on nuclear issues encountered a greater
concern in Europe because of what seemed to be Washington's
increasing preoccupation with nuclear war-fighting, rather than
pure deterrence. The Schlesinger doctrine had foreshadowed this
trend, but it was largely couched in the old values of deterrence.
The new "countervailing strategy" of the Carter Administration
promulgated in Presidential Directive 59 was perceived as a shift
(perhaps unfairly so) toward war-fighting elements as the criteria
for measuring U.S. forces. Some Europeans, particularly on the
left, saw PD 59 as the beginning of a purely counterforce doctrine,
which it was, but only partially so. Others argued that the United
States in examining nuclear war-fighting scenarios was causing an
increased risk of war, because "the unthinkable was being seriously thought about."

This uneasiness over a new American strategy had been stimulated by doubts over the efficacy of arms control in meeting Euro-

pean concerns. Even as the Carter Administration moved toward the second SALT agreement, it was clear in Europe that some of the very American weaponry (cruise missiles) needed for the European balance would be restricted by a U.S.-Soviet bargain even if only temporarily. This was the proximate cause of then-West German Chancellor Helmut Schmidt's well-known address to the International Institute for Strategic Studies (IISS) in October 1977 calling for a Euro-strategic balance.

It is important to emphasize, however, that Schmidt's call for a reexamination of the European balance was not the original impetus that eventually led to the famous dual-track NATO decision of December 1979, though it certainly contributed. The dual-track decision flowed initially from an American critique in the mid-1970s of the consequences for Europe of the declining credibility of the U.S. nuclear guarantee. The Carter Administration's program to improve conventional capabilities had also included proposals for a separate reappraisal of the theater nuclear forces. Whereas there were specific targets and goals for improving conventional defense (a three-percent rise in real spending), in the area of European nuclear weapons, the dilemma was more difficult to resolve. The status quo was no longer satisfactory to Washington or to Europe. A shift in the theater nuclear weaponry, however, would have to reassure the allies by coupling European defense to American intercontinental forces—thus requiring some new forces on the continent. A tripwire or token nuclear force might be politically palatable but would be inherently incredible as a deterrent. However, a much larger force might raise European fears that the United States hoped to confine the war to Europe. Sea-based forces in many respects were relatively preferable because of their invulnerability, but these weapons seemed too remote for political reassurance. Land-based forces would be potentially vulnerable, but would be a tangible American commitment.

Various propositions for deployment were put forward by the experts. Some suggested that an effective European force should number about 1,500 weapons, or at least no fewer than 1,000 intermediate weapons capable of reaching Soviet territory. There is no evidence that the capability of attacking Soviet territory was even challenged. NATO experts, much more sensitive to the political dimension, produced a lower range of about 200 to 600 weapons. Mindful of the neutron bomb fiasco, the United States was determined to achieve a firm consensus. Thus, in the end there was only a minimal relationship between the final numbers for deployment and such conventional military criteria as survivability or target coverage. Indeed, the final number for deployment—108 Pershing II missiles and 464 cruise missiles—was arbitrarily selected by Zbigniew Brzezinski and his staff. The higher end of the range of possibilities was chosen in order to provide fat for negotiating purposes. The second, or negotiating track, of course, was added to persuade reluctant allies to agree to the deployment track. The United States had paid a high price for the neutron bomb affair. Politics triumphed over strategy.

The point is not that the dual-track decision was wrong, but that the priorities had shifted from satisfying military requirements to the more urgent issue of calming European apprehensions by creating the second, political track. In Europe, in early 1980, there was a growing alarm over the danger of war. These fears reflected concern over the invasion of Afghanistan, the Iranian crisis, and the collapse of the SALT II treaty. The new deployment of American nuclear missiles would not proceed in the "framework" of arms control as had been anticipated by NATO, but in an atmosphere of Soviet-American confrontation. Between October 1979 and June 1980, Chancellor Schmidt had progressed from advocating the adoption of the new NATO program as a "counterweight" to the Soviet buildup, to flirting with a freeze that would suspend any Western movement toward deployment—a position that incidentally brought him into a sharp personal dispute with President Carter.

The tragedy of this period is that a reasonable and systematic effort to correct some of the military defects of the deployment of NATO's intermediate-range nuclear forces (INFs) was deflected, and then became subsumed in a new Western debate over the general strategy for dealing with Russia. What had been envisaged as two complementary, reinforcing tracks, became two conflicting tendencies. Negotiation became the antagonist of deployment. The old pillars of the Harmel Report—détente and deterrence—threatened to become opposing forces. After Afghanistan, Americans argued for tough economic sanctions and missile deployments. Europe argued for keeping open the line to Moscow. At this point other factors intruded. Both the European and American intellectual communities launched a wave of attacks on the policy of flexible response and the deployment of new missiles. Then the general public began to react against the proposed deployments. Moreover, the gap between the original NATO decision of December 1979 and the actual date for deployment in late 1983 was so extended that any decision was bound to come under a sustained attack from the Soviet Union, which in turn fed political opposition in Europe.

In the United States, the debate over nuclear strategy focused on the so-called window of vulnerability. The vulnerability of American ICBMs became a central element in the charge that the U.S. guarantee of Europe was no longer credible because the United States itself was open to a preemptive, or first strike against its own retaliatory forces. If the defense of Western Europe depended on U.S. willingness to escalate, this vulnerability of a key strategic component made the U.S. escalatory sequence implausible or extraordinarily dangerous. The long, unresolved debate over the degree of ICBM vulnerability and over the proposed MX solution could not fail to have a debilitating impact in Europe. Why should Europeans run new risks, if the Americans themselves were not willing to do so?

It was probably inevitable that the nuclear debate on both sides of the Atlantic would finally infect the psychological core of Western nuclear strategy—the threatened first-use of nuclear weapons in the face of a Soviet conventional attack. Prominent Americans not only began to attack the concept, but revealed that they had had severe doubts about the policy for many years.[1] These revelations were added to earlier expressions by American statesmen that official nuclear assurances to Europeans had been ritualistic. A crisis of confidence was unavoidable. European intellectuals echoed the American critique contending that to rely on the first-use of nuclear weapons to defend ourselves was not only "morally dubious but politically and militarily incredible." They challenged NATO solutions on the grounds that American nuclear weaponry was intended not only to deter the Soviets, but to reassure the

---

[1] McGeorge Bundy *et al.*, "Nuclear Weapons and the Atlantic Alliance," *Foreign Affairs*, Spring 1982.

allies as well. But the opposite was happening: Europeans were not reassured but increasingly concerned. Alarm was dramatically manifest by a growing anti-nuclear movement in two of the countries where deployment was most crucial, the United Kingdom and the Federal Republic of Germany. Moreover, strong sympathy for this movement was reflected in the British Labour Party and the West German Social Democratic Party.

Thus, the United States has had a weak hand to play. It was forced to negotiate, but the projected deployment of 572 missiles rested on an uncertain military rationale and the political rationale was weakening. A wide variety of combinations and numbers could be justified in the negotiations with the U.S.S.R. There was no firm base. Indeed, Soviet and American missiles were being equated—a strange distortion of the characteristic of the cruise missile, which was scarcely comparable to the SS-20. Finally, the United States had not produced any clear military doctrine to explain its new deployments.

The point to underscore is the inherent difficulties in reconciling Washington's two major objectives: to restore the credibility of Western defense, including a nuclear defense component, and to preserve a working alliance based on common policies in an era of increasing turmoil and political uncertainty in Europe. The growing clash between what the Europeans came to believe was American unilateralism and what Americans believed was European pacifism or neutralism became a vicious circle feeding on itself. Before the West German and British elections (March and June 1983), it seemed that the missile controversy might threaten the existence of NATO. Informed commentators speculated about its demise, and some even advocated it. A false dilemma was presented to American policy: either placate the Europeans by offering major concessions to the U.S.S.R., or demand the deployment of missiles as a test of Alliance solidarity, even at the expense of an Atlantic crisis. Fortunately, the Reagan Administration refused this Hobson's choice.

The strategic problems of the Alliance, however, are real ones. The United States cannot brush aside all considerations of strategy and settle for whatever combination of numbers result from bargaining in Geneva. It is not clear what level of forces is necessary for a credible deterrence. On the other hand, the United States had to make a major effort to reach a compromise at the bargaining table. A good faith effort was the price for preserving a fragile, new balance in the relationship between America and Europe, which has been reestablished only after prolonged travail. This imperative remained even in the wake of the tragic Korean airliner incident and is still valid even after the Soviet walkout from the INF negotiations last November. Despite political pressure from the right wing in America, the Reagan Administration refused to use the Geneva talks as a sanction against the U.S.S.R. Europe, of course, strongly concurred in keeping the line open, leaving the onus for disruption squarely on Moscow.

The Atrophy of an Alliance

The relative success of the United States and the Atlantic allies in collaborating to deal with the military aspects of the new era of strategic parity has not been paralleled by a similar success in political relations. The trend has been in the opposite direction. Since 1973 the United States and Europe have been drifting apart. By 1982, during the Reagan Administration's attack on the proposed Soviet-European gas pipeline, relations reached a low point. This disarray necessarily eroded the U.S. ability to manage the politics of the missile deployments.

There are underlying causes for this remarkable deterioration of the most successful of peacetime alliances. The first has been the natural tendency of the older great powers in Europe to reclaim some freedom of action from the tutelage of the United States. This is an old trend, grown stronger. Initially, the European aspiration for a new collective identity was received in Washington with considerable understanding and sympathy. But gradually a more hostile reaction set in. Americans saw Europeans as seeking the military protection of the United States, but not accepting the burden of responding to the U.S.S.R. either in Europe or, especially, in the Third World.

The readjustment of power with an alliance is a natural historical process. And this could have easily been accomplished in NATO, despite strains caused by the French. But the constellation of factors that encouraged a process of adjustment began to change. The failure of the "Year of Europe," in 1973-74, however misconceived by the United States or mismanaged on both sides, left a bitter residue in the United States. It seemed to many American observers to reflect a cynical Europe distancing itself from America's domestic troubles. After the humiliation of the final days of Vietnam, Europe came to see the United States as a "factor of uncertainty." The 1976 election year proved to be only an interlude before relations exploded again, this time over the neutron bomb.

Again the neutron bomb affair was rationalized as a misunderstanding—but it also reflected growing European doubts over American military strategy. For the United States, one result was a greater determination to proceed meticulously in consulting the Europeans at each stage in the planning that led to the dual-track decision of December 1979. Yet the closeness of the consultations was deceptive; it masked a further deterioration in relations, stimulated in part by personal antipathies between Carter and Schmidt, but aggravated more fundamentally by the gap between the United States and Europe in their appreciation of the international situation.

Détente in Europe had become a permanently operating factor, not subject to reversal except for the most serious of causes. In the United States there was an incipient revolt against détente; it later flowered in the Reagan consensus. The drastic shock of the invasion of Afghanistan and the Iranian seizure of the hostages revived the European-American conflict over East-West strategy. The United States took the invasion as a major departure in Soviet policy—an ominous harbinger of a new Soviet aggressiveness. Sanctions against the U.S.S.R. were a minimal reaction as the Americans saw it. Both the West German and French leaders, however, conducted themselves in a baffling manner; they raced to conciliate then-Soviet President Leonid Brezhnev, which appeared to many Americans to be not far from outright appeasement. The new split with Europe was symbolized by an acrimonious encounter between Jimmy Carter and Helmut Schmidt in a private meeting during the Venice summit in June 1980. Even allowing for the mercurial temperament of the West German leader, it would have been inconceivable for such a dangerous fissure to develop between these two particular allies, unless there was a strong undercurrent in the Federal Republic that made Schmidt's performance consonant with a West German desire to be seen as distancing itself from the United States. Matters worsened. There was a new split over Poland when Premier Wojciech Jaruzelski imposed martial law. The Europeans argued *realpolitik* and cited Yalta as justification for their lack of response. After an initial hesitation, the Reagan Administration produced an even greater crisis in June 1982 with its insistence on a policy of selective sanctions against the U.S.S.R. The gas pipeline dispute may have struck Europeans as needlessly punitive (if not hypocritical) in light of resumed American grain sales. But the United States was dismayed and embittered by the insistent European rationalizations of Soviet pressures, first in Afghanistan, and then in Poland.

What was at issue was not simply whether to impose sanctions, but the larger question of the nature of the threat from the East and how to deal with it. Out of the myriad issues in dispute, two questions seem to have become commanding ones: first, whether arms control should be subordinate to other aspects of the East-West struggle (i.e., linkage of Poland to the Geneva talks) or treated independently; and second whether the Western Alliance should apply a policy of increasing pressures (i.e., the gas pipeline sanctions) or seek a progressive reconciliation with the U.S.S.R.

The split between Europe and the United States over the role of arms control has become increasingly serious. The Europeans are worried that the decoupling of the American strategic deterrent from the European forces means that a war could conceivably be confined to Europe. While seeking to redress the European balance as well as recouple American forces to the continent, the Europeans place much greater emphasis on an accommodation through arms control. Indeed, they see an agreement as vastly preferable in light of their own domestic political pressures. A simple military response to the Soviet Union no longer commands strong support in most of Europe. But arms control is an area dominated by the two superpowers. There is no clear role for Europe. In the first phase of SALT this was a manageable problem. Then America found it difficult to conduct private negotiations with Moscow if each move required a lengthy debate in Brussels. Europe acquiesced to a spectator's role. Subsequently, Europe found that its security was more and more subject to indirect bargaining between the two superpowers (i.e., "gray area" systems which were not truly intercontinental; but by virtue of deployment in Europe or at sea they could cover large target areas yet were not eligible for SALT negotiations). Hence, Schmidt's complaint in his October 1977 IISS speech calling for a Euro-strategic balance.

Moreover, the Europeans finally agreed to and supported the deployment of Pershing IIs and cruise missiles in the context of a continuing arms control process closely related to SALT III. When the United States suspended the process in January 1980 in retaliation for the invasion of Afghanistan, Europe found itself committed to a potential confrontation with the U.S.S.R. without having had a real voice in the decision. Consequently, the Europeans pressed both the Soviet Union and the United States to begin negotiations about theater nuclear weapons as a safety valve to relieve growing tensions, even though it made little sense to proceed with an INF negotiation if the SALT process itself was destined to expire. The American reaction to European pressures was predictable: irritation under Carter gave way under Reagan to a deeper American resentment over the lack of a common appreciation of the Soviet threat. The Reagan Administration in any case was skeptical of arms control negotiations and had no plan; it grudgingly agreed to INF talks.

Largely out of a desire to halt the deterioration of European opinion, the United States then selected the most dramatic negotiating opener, but the one least likely to lead to any agreement, the zero option. Far from being placated, some Europeans regarded the offer as hypocritical, and they concluded that the Reagan Administration was, in fact, hostile to arms control. The projected deployments to redress a gross imbalance had raised fears that it was part of an effort to reestablish American superiority by devising a first strike or "decapitation" strategy to be executed from European bases. Since there was no particular doctrine to justify all of the deployments (especially the Pershing II capability), the Reagan Administration increasingly came to regard the missile deployment as a test of Alliance loyalty.

On a broader level, there was also an increasing divergence. To both Presidents Carter and Reagan, the Europeans began to appear more and more as the honest brokers between Moscow and Washington: the British in Afghanistan, the Germans in arms control, and the French in Central America. Where the Europeans saw opportunities for accommodation, the Reagan Administration saw the possibility for a more aggressive counterpolicy against the U.S.S.R., designed to increase internal economic pressures which would build over time to a point that the Soviet leaders would have no choice but to adopt a far-reaching liberalization. Thus Western pressures were not designed to affect the external behavior of the U.S.S.R.—the traditional rationale for Western policy—but to affect internal change. Without basic internal changes, it was argued, there was little likelihood of an international accommodation because Soviet foreign policy was a product of the domestic structure.

For Europe this attitude threatened a radical turn in American policy. It was resisted, not because Europe was wedded to Soviet natural gas, or even because of the difficult impact of the economic recession of 1982. European resistance ran much deeper: for Europe, the Soviet Union remained a potential negotiating partner in stabilizing the continent. Moscow's demands, if exceedingly difficult, were nevertheless tractable. The likelihood of a Soviet attack was receding. Poland was an example of the Soviet difficulty in pursuing the old Stalinist solutions in Eastern Europe. For Europe, the Soviet Union was a "fumbling giant," caught up by serious internal and external troubles. While conceding that Moscow could indeed be a dangerous and aggressive adversary, the Europeans saw the Western task as limiting the conflict rather than exacerbating it by confrontation and especially by intervention in remote regions. It was the purpose of Western policy to encourage the elements of restraint—trade and arms control in particular. If the United States jeopardized this approach it would provoke a major conflict within the Alliance.

Americans argued that this was a Euro-centric view of a contest that was truly global. Failure to deal with challenges outside Europe would eventually erode the Alliance's ability to manage the central conflict in Europe itself. Moreover, arms control could not be pursued simply in the name of détente or as a safety valve to relieve pressures; it had to have a militarily significant content and be linked to general Soviet behavior. Economic relations were a critical element of linkage and Western leverage. Europeans saw (and see) the primary task as managing Soviet decline, while Americans saw the task as encouraging, if not accelerating, it.

The American performance in this debate has been uneven. On the one hand, the gas pipeline dispute was ended with an American retreat (if not a rout). Moreover, the punitive policy advocated by some in the Reagan Administration was tempered by a growing pragmatism in 1983. It is no longer clear what the general strategy of the Administration will be. The anti-communist, philosophical underpinnings of President Reagan's beliefs have not been shaken. They were sharpened by the Korean airliner disaster. But the Administration has demonstrated much greater operational flexibility since the pipeline confrontation. The initial reaction to the Korean incident was surprisingly restrained. But the rhetorical response was strident and seemed to revive the early ideological tone. The incident also revived pressures for a harsher policy on economic relations as well as pressures against arms control.

On the deeper Alliance issues, the European dissent has strengthened the views of conservatives in America who see a dwindling area of common interests with Europe. Indeed, what began as a questioning of European policies on specific issues has spread to a questioning of the value of the entire Alliance. On both the right and the left, it is being argued that U.S. interests are no longer served by the continuation of the Alliance. If, for example, Europe will not support the deployment of American nuclear weapons, then it would be unconscionable to continue stationing American forces in Europe; Europe and America should simply agree to go their separate ways. The ominous aspect of this trend was its political origins. It was lodged increasingly among those conservative elements in America that hitherto have been the most resolute anti-communists. But this disaffection from Europe has not been confined to the American political right. It is found among more liberal constituencies as well. The breadth of this anti-European reaction is clearly underrated in Europe.

As a parallel, in Europe there seems to be growing disenchantment with the Reagan Administration. Some Europeans now openly advocate decreasing dependence on the United States. Many express a renewed interest in an independent political entity, which must necessarily have anti-Atlanticist definition; and some toy with the notion of a separate nuclear deterrent. Europeans appear to believe that somehow they can reduce their dependence on the United States without stimulating American neoisolationist sentiment. They argue that the United States has no viable option other than the commitment to Europe. Yet, without a common evaluation of the East-West contest, which remains at the heart of the Alliance's rationale and is the justification for its enormous and costly military effort, the trend toward separation between America and Europe is likely to continue. Each turn of the contest with Moscow could accelerate the separation.

What is at stake for the United States is quite clear. After the Second World War, the United States executed a historical reversal of policy, ending its isolation and joining Europe in a long-term alliance to contain Soviet power. Tying the United States to the defense of the continent was the real significance of the creation of NATO. The second achievement was drawing the Federal Republic of Germany back into the European concert. Indeed, the conciliation (and containment) of West Germany came to be implicit objectives of the Alliance. It is precisely these achievements that are the potential victims of the current struggle. The Soviet Union hopes to separate the United States from Europe, and to separate the Federal Republic from its Western orientation. As the stronger partner, it is incumbent on the United States to halt the drift in Atlantic relations and if necessary, to make concessions to the European view. It is a question not of sentiment, but of self-interest. The only conceivable long-term resolution of the East-West struggle is Soviet accommodation with a permanently adverse balance of power. The essential ingredient of that balance is the European-American alliance.

The foregoing suggests strongly that the Europeans are indeed right: the United States has no grand alternative to the present course. But America cannot live with a crippled defense or with a crippled Alliance. Both have to be repaired. It is also important that these aims not be pursued at the expense of the longer term opportunities to improve Soviet-American relations, either with excessive belligerence or conciliation.

Soviet Political and Military Aims

Soviet intentions in Europe have been remarkably consistent: to preserve its East European gains while striving for greater influence in Western Europe. Priority, of course, has always been accorded to preserving its empire, but the U.S.S.R. has never settled for a simple status quo. Its strategy has been to exploit Western acquiescence to the status quo in Eastern Europe in order to gain leverage over Western freedom of action. Thus, the struggle for Europe has always had two dimensions: first, the incessant demand that the division of the continent be formally recognized; but, second, the crude manipulation of that recognition to make West European policy subject to a Soviet veto. This has been persistently applied in Germany. It is no accident that Soviet President Yuri Andropov warned of a "palisade" of missiles that would separate the two German states—an image calculated to pit German national aspirations against the requirements of Western security.

The Alliance has proved itself able to cope with Soviet tactics in Europe, though not outside the NATO area. And it has done so largely on the basis of a balance of power that was favorable to the West. It was the U.S.S.R. that was the *demandeur*, the supplicant seeking Western confirmation of the legitimacy of its presence in Eastern Europe. In the mid-1970s the situation began to change. Soviet minimum demands were largely satisfied by the German treaties of Willy Brandt, and by the broad pan-European confirmation of the Soviet position at Helsinki in 1975. But the expected gains for the Soviet Union from these major strides forward turned out to be marginal. Détente with the United States foundered and the "Finlandization" of Europe made little progress. When faced with the realities of its own military disengagement in Eastern Europe, Moscow could not afford the risks; hence the bargain of trading a reduction in U.S. nuclear weapons in Europe for withdrawal of Soviet troops, as suggested in the Mutual and Balanced Force Reduction (MBFR) negotiations in Vienna, was never accepted. The very solution that the U.S.S.R. was to press so strongly in 1980-81—the freeze on nuclear deployment—had been brushed aside in Vienna from 1975 to 1977 when it was proposed by the West (and known as "Option 3"). It was never that simple, of course, but in retrospect it appears to have been a major Soviet blunder.

It is against this background that the decision to proceed with the SS-20 deployments becomes more understandable. The U.S.S.R. began to realize that the fruits of détente would not flourish autonomously; there would have to be continuing Soviet installment payments to the West. The United States, for example, was demanding a substantial restriction on Soviet strategic forces in SALT. The Europeans were pressing for genuine concessions on human rights and intra-European relations; the United States, under Carter, joined the human rights campaign. Clearly, the Europeans and the Americans had to be pressured, and the precise instrument of intimidation was the SS-20.

There are several additional interpretations of the SS-20 deployment. One argues that the Soviet rationale should be taken more or less at face value—i.e., largely a modernization of an aging, obsolete force; a modernization in which the overall force was replaced on roughly a one-for-one basis. It could also be argued that the explanation for this behavior lies in the bureaucratic politics in the Kremlin. A major program once begun is almost impossible to reverse. It could be that Brezhnev, in political maneuvering involving his successors, chose not to challenge or test his political position in a debate over a military program.

Whatever the technical motives for the deployment, it also seems likely that the Soviet Union sought to change radically the European balance and the European perception of that balance. The deployment of SS-20s began in 1976-77, when there was still a modicum of détente. The deployment program proceeded without interruption even though the United States and the U.S.S.R. resumed the SALT II negotiations in 1977 and signed the treaty in June 1979. Nothing in the Western posture, including British and French strategic plans, justified the scale or pace of the Soviet effort. At no point did the U.S.S.R. seek a genuine discussion, let alone an accommodation on the SS-20 program. Indeed, throughout the period leading to the NATO dual-track decision of December 1979, the Soviets made no effort even to engage the United States on the European situation despite numerous logical openings. In particular there was a clear opportunity in June 1979 at the Vienna summit, when President Carter submitted a long agenda of possible arms control initiatives that included initiation of discussion of weapons not yet covered by SALT. Brezhnev rejected it. Not until the very eve of the NATO decision did the U.S.S.R. belatedly begin to react, but only by offering a version of a highly advantageous freeze. By then it was too late to affect the initial

NATO decision. Even then the Soviets did not in fact freeze deployments. The subsequent phase suggests that the Soviets wished to impose a major humiliation on both the United States and Western Europe by defeating the proposed dual-track program. There was only a sporadic effort at negotiation accompanied by an increasingly shrill effort to blackmail the United States and its allies.

In their counterattack against NATO's dual-track decision, the Soviets advanced three major arguments: (1) that a balance of medium-range forces exists in Europe; (2) that American plans for deploying the Pershing II missile would force a change in Soviet strategy to deal with the danger of a "suprise suppression" of Soviet command and control; and (3) the Far East was a separate theater, a legitimate security concern, not subject to U.S.-Soviet bargaining.

The problem of measuring the balance in Europe is, of course, an old debate. The Soviets rest their case on the inclusion of the French and British nuclear forces and the inclusion of U.S. aircraft, such as the F-4; this skews the NATO figures upward. And, naturally, the Soviets reduce their own side of the ledger so that the balance comes out about even at roughly 1,000 systems. In the course of the negotiations the Soviets have argued that these balances could be reduced to 600 and then to 300 systems. Later Andropov acknowledged that counting warheads as well as delivery systems could be adopted. But the Soviets subsequently calculated the Western forces, including the British and French "potential" at maximum capabilities (i.e., assuming some of the British and French forces would be equipped with multiple independently-targetable reentry vehicles, or MIRVs) so that the outcome would be about even. All of this is simply a subterfuge to conceal the major aim of excluding any American missile deployments whatsoever. In the wake of the Korean airliner affair, the Soviets bluntly reasserted their opposition to any American deployments, whether cruise missiles or Pershing IIs, even while toying with the numbers of reduced SS-20s.

The Soviet missile force currently in European Russia is believed to be 243 launchers, or 729 warheads—i.e., roughly the size of the force deployed in the U.S.S.R. (in SS-4 and SS-5 missiles) for several decades. This is surely no coincidence; it suggests that the prospect for a major drawdown of Soviet missile forces is not very promising without significant political compensation.

Another Soviet factor is the new importance of the Far East. The Soviets began redeploying some short- and medium-range nuclear forces to the Far East in the 1970s. The Far East subsequently became a distinct theater for operations with a new independent command. The number of SS-20s deployed in the Far Eastern command has been 108 launchers, or 324 warheads. (There is no proclaimed freeze on deployments in this area.) The Soviets argue that the separation between European Russia and the Far East is legitimate and reflects a genuine security concern—a concern about China that has been dramatically expressed to several American presidents. To include the Far East deployments in U.S.-Soviet negotiations would thus involve Soviet concessions to the United States for the benefit of China—a highly unlikely Soviet bargain. The Soviets have proposed to dismantle any missiles and launchers reduced in Europe, implying a freeze in the Far East. The Far Eastern factor thus sets a sharp limit on Soviet freedom to negotiate. It is difficult to imagine any Soviet leader agreeing to reductions in Brezhnev's Far Eastern buildup merely to placate the United States. Surely, this is not a very likely prospect for a new Soviet leadership. At best, the Far Eastern deployments might be frozen. This seems to be the net effect of proposals made by Andropov on August 27 and by Reagan at the United Nations on September 26, 1983. The United States countered Andropov's offer to dismantle missiles by proposing a separate ceiling for intermediate-range missiles outside of Europe that the United States would in practice not reach, although it would retain the right to do so.

There are shrill Soviet claims of a special threat of a surprise attack because of the short flight time of the Pershing II missile in Europe. Is the Soviet concern a serious one, or merely advanced for bargaining purposes? Does the Soviet General Staff truly believe that the United States would begin a general nuclear attack by first launching the Pershing II missiles? This would have the effect of providing about 15 minutes warning that an ICBM attack had also been launched and a strong confirmation of a general attack. (A separate attack of 100 Pershings is too foolish to contemplate.) Moreover, the Pershing's range is too limited to attack all Soviet command and control centers. It could not even attack all of the SS-20 sites. The Pershing II differs only slightly from the Poseidon missiles that have been stationed on submarines patrolling the European area. Yet an analysis of Soviet pronouncements, military writings and exercises suggests a strong concern over the presence of American nuclear missiles in West Germany. Indeed, the best case for the deterrent value of the U.S. program is made by the Soviet military.

There is also the political dimension: the American deployment is the first serious threat from West German territory capable of reaching well into the U.S.S.R. Andropov has called attention to this rather dramatically. Moreover, the Pershing II deployment does alter the character of the American threat. Even if it only adds marginally (50 separate attacks of two warheads per target against hardened targets), it has to be dealt with by Soviet defense planners, either by plans for rapid preemption, by relocation of command and control, or by defensive measures, e.g., super-hardening. All things considered, eliminating (or severely limiting) the Pershing II through bargaining must be a highly attractive and inexpensive option.

The Soviet argument about taking into account the French and British systems is more difficult to take seriously; not because they are of no strategic value but because the Soviet leaders surely know that they have in fact been compensated in the previous SALT bargaining. By their own admission they regarded the unequal levels of submarine-launched ballistic missiles (SLBMs) in SALT I as compensation for the British and French SLBMs. At the time of the SALT I signing in May 1972, they issued a unilateral statement to this effect, which the United States duly rebutted. At Vladivostok in 1974 the Soviets dropped a specific demand for new compensation in the SALT II framework. They did so as part of a general agreement that the levels would be equal: 2,400 strategic vehicles, and 1,320 MIRVed missiles. The United States withdrew proposals for unequal MIRV levels to compensate for overall inequality, and then dropped demands for cuts in Soviet heavy missiles. The Soviets dropped their demands to count U.S. forward-based aircraft and the French and British submarine missiles, and to bar U.S. air-launched missiles. Therefore, through the termination date for SALT II (1985) at least, the Soviets have no case for compensation for British or French forces. Their position is largely for bargaining purposes, though again, after the Korean airliner crisis, they have hardened their public stance. However, they have hinted that the British and French forces had two "faces," strategic and European, suggesting they might accept a proposal to put these forces under the Strategic Arms Reduction Talks (START). A rather strange episode occurred in late November 1983 when the Soviet negotiator seemed to suggest that discussion of the British and French forces be shifted to the START forum; it was officially denied in Moscow, but suspicions remain.

In sum, the core of the Soviet position seems to suggest that there is only slight flexibility, some interest in reducing Soviet SS-20 forces in Europe, little chance for similar reductions in the Far East, but probably some concern about removing the Pershing II threat. These narrow boundaries explain why the U.S.S.R. moved glacially in the Geneva talks. (A political crisis in the Kremlin may have hampered the usual last-minute Soviet bargaining.)

The military aspect, however, has never monopolized Soviet policy in Europe. The Soviets are deeply interested in weakening the solidarity of the Western Alliance and, in particular, weakening the West German-American axis. Until the spring of 1983, the Soviets relied heavily on the West German Social Democrats to oppose the American deployments. It is interesting to note that during the summer of 1982, when the controversy over the gas pipeline was most intense, the Soviets were relatively inactive on the INF issues (passing up the initiatives of Paul Nitze). Only after the collapse of Schmidt's coalition, and Brezhnev's death, did the Soviets launch a new diplomatic campaign.

The Soviets probably no longer expect to reverse the deployments, especially after the shooting down of the Korean airliner. What they have to decide is whether to tolerate some deployment under the rubric of an eventual agreement, thus softening an outright political defeat, or to monitor the deployment in its early stages in 1984, keeping up the political pressure and adopting some countermeasures, and then decide whether a favorable bargain could still be struck. The choice rests in large part on a greater decision: whether the Andropov regime wishes to ease its relations with the United States and preserve some measure of European détente, or confront the United States and await a change in Western policy perhaps some years hence. The impact of the Korean airliner incident has been to move Soviet policy toward this more strident posture. The withdrawal from the negotiations was another step toward a tougher stance.

The Negotiating Record

The INF negotiations have been bizarre.

The United States, having decided in 1979 that NATO's strategic dilemma required a major new missile deployment, offered to cancel it in 1981, if the Soviets dismantled all of their SS-20s— which was only one of the causes of the original NATO decision. This zero option could have created a serious problem, leaving the U.S.S.R. free to deploy an unlimited number of shorter range weapons against most European targets, but barring the United States from any new weapons capable of attacking Soviet territory. The new tactical imbalance in Europe would make any nuclear exchange virtually suicidal for West Germany. Even if the United States had compensated by shifting its cruise missile deployment to sea-based systems, NATO would have lost the tangible coupling with American strategic forces.

To be sure, the zero option was clever public relations and did indeed put the U.S.S.R. on the defensive; there was, moreover, no risk that the Soviets would emulate the Duke of York. They did not build up their SS-20s only to tear all of them down. Nevertheless, the zero option raised some serious questions about the lack of strategy and doctrine underlying the American deployment. The American missiles were apparently more of a bargaining chip than a response to a serious military deterioration. Subsequent U.S. offers in 1983 ranged from as low as 50 warheads to a high of 450 and a final offer of 420, thus underscoring the purely political character of the proposed American deployment.

In light of this, the famous "walk in the woods," (the private conversation between Paul Nitze and Yuli Kvitsinsky in July 1982) remains highly puzzling. Probably it will never be fully understood unless there is more evidence available from the Soviet side. In any case, the American terms were shrewdly drawn by Nitze and seemed to reflect a realistic analysis of the Soviet position, though based on perhaps too pessimistic a projection of weakening European support. Its essence was to abandon the Pershing II missile, in return for a Soviet reduction to an equal level (about 300 warheads) in Europe (actually 75 *land-based* cruise missile launchers with four missiles each for the U.S. and 75 SS-20 launchers with three warheads each for the U.S.S.R.). In the Far East the United States would accept a freeze on Soviet deployments at the then-current level (then 90 launchers, but now 117). In return, the Soviets would drop their claim for compensation for the British and French intermediate-range nuclear systems. Altogether a sound and sensible proposition in the light of two factors: (1) the U.S. deployments of 75 launchers would serve the military rationale which had already become quite vague; and (2) the United States risked losing the entire deployment if European opinion continued to turn hostile, as seemed probable in the summer of 1982.

Moscow's long silence after the walk in the woods is suspicious. If, as later claimed, the Soviets were appalled or perplexed by a purely personal approach, why did they allow more than 60 days to pass without contacting the Americans? The doctrine is that silence implies consent. Had the United States supported the Nitze proposal wholeheartedly, how would the Soviets have handled it? One suspects that the Soviets were indeed interested, but probably calculated that there would still be time to settle at this price later. Meanwhile, the strife between the United States and Europe might make Soviet concessions unnecessary. The subsequent Soviet hints about reviving the Nitze-Kvitsinsky offer that surfaced in various channels in the summer of 1983 would seem to confirm that Moscow regarded it as still roughly negotiable. After the clash over the Korean airliner shoot-down, the Soviets seemed to repudiate hints along the lines of another Nitze-Kvitsinsky bargain.

American conduct is also baffling. The reasoning for the White House not accepting the Nitze package is not easy to understand. The initial reaction was apparently favorable, but the final decision was a rejection (though couched as a willingness to keep open the channel). One argument was American concern for the impact on Schmidt's political position at that time; this is unconvincing. He probably would have supported a compromise without question had he actually been asked. (He has since confirmed this.) Why the Soviets were not contacted privately in this period is also not clear. There was, no doubt, pique in the Pentagon (and perhaps in the White House) over Nitze's boldness. Subsequent U.S. behavior suggests that the critical substantive issue was the offer to sacrifice the Pershing II missile, which one important American offical described as the "keystone" of the entire deployment. Removing the keystone was obviously objectionable. In later negotiating sessions the United States has offered numbers for ceilings that would embrace the Nitze proposal, but it has thus far insisted on retaining the freedom to choose any mix of missiles on the NATO side, i.e., to include some level of Pershings. It may well be that the entire episode will be seen as an important lost opportunity.

In any case, the United States was forced to abandon the zero option as it began to lose credibility in Europe and as the Europeans became more uneasy about confronting public opposition in the spring of 1983. Few in Europe believed that the zero option was a genuine negotiating proposal. An American rescue operation was staged, beginning with a trip by Vice President George Bush and ending with a new, flexible U.S. offer to settle on virtually any number short of the planned deployment, but clearly with an equal global ceiling. The Soviets promptly rejected it to avoid making the same error they had made earlier in reacting too sluggishly to the zero option. The Soviets surfaced a variant that adopted the principle of counting warheads, and vaguely tied the Soviet level to the level of British and French missiles (162), but still squeezing out any new American deployment. The Europeans were intrigued: "the best news from Moscow in a long time."[2] Not to be outflanked, the U.S. promptly rejected it. In the wake of these predictable moves, the endgame began to take shape. Inevitably, speculation focused on the formulas initiated in the Nitze-Kvitsinsky bargain. The new West German government, while insisting on its steadfast determination to deploy, made it clear that it would be willing to consider a settlement along the lines of the Nitze-Kvitsinsky equation. The United States, however, was still worried about West German opinion and resisted moving in a direction that would eliminate the Pershing II deployment. Washington seemed to lag behind the changing political situation. The

---

[2] *The Economist*, May 7, 1983.

government of Helmut Kohl was committed to deployment, and missing the Pershing deadline in West Germany would no longer be a key test. Indeed, there was much to be said for beginning the deployments with British and Italian increments of cruise missiles, and not subjecting West Germany to such an early confrontation, which could still spread to intra-German matters.

Still, the effect of the Korean airliner disaster was to cast a shadow over the negotiations. Both sides seemed to harden their posture. The prospects for a Reagan-Andropov summit seemed to have been cut short; without this incentive the chances of concession on either side receded. A new stalemate loomed even though both sides advanced new, last-minute proposals concerning the British and French systems as well as deployments in the Far East. On November 23, 1983, the Soviet negotiating team withdrew. Moscow announced the end of its moratorium on SS-20s and warned of countermeasures.

Future Policy

NATO's policy is basically sound. Despite some flaws, the dual track is the only alternative and should be pursued. The precise tactics are variable. No one outside the confines of the governments involved can prescribe the maneuvers that may be called for over the next year or so. But the essence of the policy is clear.

First, NATO must proceed with a *significant* deployment of American nuclear missile forces in Europe. Whether this force must include a mix of both Pershing IIs and cruise missiles or must be deployed within prescribed deadlines is in part a function of the political and negotiating dynamics. The deployment of Pershing II missiles, because of their hard target capabilities and quick reaction time would be militarily preferable. Their abandonment in return for significant Soviet concessions is conceivable, however. What is surely not acceptable is a pathetic token deployment of American missiles (i.e., 50). That would be a military and political debacle. The long-term consequences of such an outcome would soon return to haunt both the United States and its allies. The Soviet threat would be largely unaffected, recoupling would not be firmly achieved, and few would believe in the determination of the United States. Such a further blow to a credible defense posture would only stimulate more radical solutions—the freeze, or no-first-use, or even a significant disengagement of American forces. The numbers involved in the Nitze-Kvitsinsky exchange (i.e., about 300 warheads) seem roughly acceptable as an outcome.

Deployment is not an end in itself. It will not end the crisis of confidence within the Alliance, nor completely repair the defects of military strategy. But it is likely to be an emotional turning point for the Alliance. If deployment proceeds, regardless of public demonstrations and protests, the succeeding phase is likely to be politically more manageable. If the Soviets resume negotiations, then much of the heat will be drained from the issue.

If, however, negotiations remain suspended and the Soviets initiate some counterdeployments, it will be imperative that NATO maintain a solid front. The more so, since the full American deployment will stretch over several years. Deployment in the Netherlands and Belgium will still be open to debate in their parliaments. It would be a serious setback, though not fatal, if these two smaller allies were to reject any missile deployments. For this reason, the long-term political negotiating position of the United States must be especially convincing. This means a willingness to stop deployment at a point where an accommodation is possible. A new offer to dramatize this position might be wise, though the venomous atmosphere militates against new U.S. flexibility. In any case, the United States needs to make it clear that, if negotiations completely founder, it is the responsibility of the U.S.S.R. NATO must be careful, however, that it does not slip into a position of offering to denuclearize Belgium and Holland simply because deployments there have not yet begun. And in no circumstances should the United States offer to take British and French weapons into consideration in these INF negotiations. This would be the start of a nuclear Finlandization, of matching Europe alone with the U.S.S.R.

As deployment begins, it might be advisable to consider some alternatives, including a merger of the START and INF negotiations. It has always been an attractive idea and could be considered as a face-saving compromise to avoid a final breakdown in the INF negotiations. It would end the artificial distinction between U.S.-European weapons and intercontinental ones. It would effectively counter Soviet divisive tactics over the British and French systems. Leaving these forces out entirely and indefinitely from all East-West negotiations seems implausible. To do so risks some day setting Britain and France against their non-nuclear allies, including West Germany. One side-benefit might well be to inspire a greater sense of Atlantic unity in the face of new broader negotiations.

There are some strategic problems. The United States would probably find that under any broad arms control scheme it would have to reduce its own missile forces, in order to accommodate the expansion of British and French forces, which are scheduled to grow significantly with the advent of the French M-4 submarine-launched ballistic missile and the British adoption of the Trident system. A merger of INF-START might mean that subsequently British and French forces could no longer be portrayed as primarily or exclusively for the defense of their homelands, but would have to be regarded as available for the defense of the integrity of the NATO area. The French probably would not agree, and would not yield to inducements to enter into joint targeting or other strategic planning. The British might be more amenable. The mere fact of negotiations with the U.S.S.R., however, would stimulate some implicit consideration of a combined strategic force.

In post-deployment Europe, there is likely to be a continuing and perhaps even stronger aversion to nuclear weapons. A serious problem is the near obsession with strengthening conventional defense championed by a broad spectrum in the United States and Europe as a means of reducing dependence on nuclear weapons. Conventional defense has become the panacea for NATO problems and the respectable justification for nearly every anti-nuclear assault. The current cliché is that nuclear strength cannot substitute for conventional weapons and forces. But the obverse—that conventional forces can substitute for the deterrent function of nuclear weapons—is not automatically valid. The dilemma will remain: Soviet conventional forces are likely to be stronger than NATO's in the only truly critical area, Central Europe. Geography favors the Soviet Union. Politics dictate the forward defense of West Germany, but its territory is extremely vulnerable to a quick thrust which would have the political consequence of leaving one third of West Germany behind Soviet lines. This would be a revolutionary gain for the U.S.S.R. It has to be prevented beforehand.

Western deterrence of this potentially tempting prospect can never rest on conventional forces alone, no matter how strong. The U.S.S.R. will never be completely convinced that it could not mass sufficent forces to break through at some point. And of course, there is no guarantee that the U.S.S.R. would not use tactical nuclear weapons to blast a hole in Western defenses. How would a conventional defense force then respond?

The idea of many Europeans is that the 250,000 American troops are a hostage and a sufficent deterrent to the Soviet Union. This is a questionable guarantee. After all, the United States has fought two wars with non-nuclear powers, in Korea and Vietnam, and suffered nearly 100,000 casualties without using a single nuclear weapon. The presence in Europe and adjacent waters of some intermediate-range nuclear forces under American (or even NATO) command, remains essential to any effective concept of extended deterrence. Failure to preserve this concept in the current contest with the U.S.S.R. could be very dangerous even if compensated by massive increases in conventional defense, which are unlikely in any case.

What is true of the intermediate-range nuclear forces is, however, not equally applicable to shorter range forces. Battlefield weapons have a waning military rationale and carry an increasingly high political price. The use of short-range weapons against East German territory is never likely to be acceptable to any West German government. The continuing presence of most of these weapons raises questions about NATO strategy (or the lack thereof) that should remain quiescent, i.e., would the United States try to fight a limited nuclear war on a European battlefield? Such constant questioning is destructive to alliance relationships and presents a dangerously misleading countenance for the Soviets to confront. In consequence, for political and psychological reasons, there should be a scaling-down and withdrawal of most tactical weapons. This could be negotiated with the Soviets, but preferably should be unilateral in order to strengthen the arguments against the anti-nuclear movements. There would still remain the Soviet dimension, because it appears that the U.S.S.R. intends to modernize its short-range nuclear forces with a new generation. If so, there may be another crisis in a few years. Someone is bound to argue that the Soviets will use their short-range system on the battlefield daring the United States to counter, either against allied territory, or to escalate with all its attendant risks. It would therefore be wise for the United States to retain or deploy a select number of systems (modern Pershing Is) that could be stationed further from the front but could still attack second-echelon targets in Eastern Europe. There are NATO studies on this issue, which will probably come before the political authorities in the near future.

Finally, there is the question of doctrine. Flexible response remains the best of the alternatives. In the present atmosphere it obviously cannot be replaced by one that emphasizes a greater reliance on nuclear weapons. But it also cannot be replaced by a doctrine of conventional response and no-first-use of nuclear weapons without risking the long-term neutralization of Western Europe. If Europe is cut loose from the American nuclear force by a new policy, it must inevitably seek re-insurance in the East.

The foregoing measures may go some distance in alleviating Atlantic differences without sacrificing defense policy, but it leaves open the longer term issue of treating with the U.S.S.R. For this, a new long-term strategy is obviously needed, and badly needed. The INF talks could eventually lead to an agreement, in which case the Alliance would need a strategy to exploit this breakthrough. Or, the negotiations could fail altogether, and a period of much greater tension would ensue. In either case, the Alliance needs a single, agreed policy on overall relations with the Soviet Union.

To achieve this, both the United States and its European partners will need to make some concessions and compromises. The United States, for its part, must temper its Manichaean view of the contest and try to smooth its fluctuations from one extreme to another in dealing with the U.S.S.R. when administrations change in Washington. The Europeans, for their part, must acknowledge that détente is indivisible, and cannot be applied only in Europe. Both must agree that challenges outside the NATO area are of common concern, no matter how seemingly remote. This does not necessarily mean European action, but it does require an agreed analysis and, probably, a united front. Both sides need to recognize that some economic intercourse between East and West is unavoidable and should be managed rather than debated. Finally, there has to be a linkage between security and arms control. The

United States needs to overcome its sporadic antipathy toward arms control, and the Europeans need to rid themselves of the notion that there is an arms control solution to every security problem.

In short, NATO needs to settle on a centrist policy.

If this is achieved, the longer term prospects for the Alliance are reasonably promising. The breakdown in the Soviet empire in Eastern Europe, the vulnerabilities along its periphery in the south and east, plus severe problems at home are strong incentives for seeking a period of respite. The indefinite expansion of the U.S.S.R. is not historically inevitable, no matter what the trends of Russian history. There are many reasons to believe that the Soviet empire forged after World War II has passed its apogee, even though the Soviet military machine grows stronger. An aggressive Western policy of accelerating this decline will risk a collision with the hard core of Russian nationalism. And the resistance will be fierce. A passive policy, awaiting history's verdict, risks a Soviet recovery—if not immediately, in the decades to come. The Europeans are right when they portray the U.S.S.R. as a "fumbling giant," but they need to recognize a giant nevertheless. The Americans are right when they see the aggressive bear clawing its way outward, but the United States needs to recognize it is a power not without limits. For each vision the requirements for Western policy are about the same: a viable military balance in major categories, a unified Alliance capable of resisting Soviet thrusts in Europe and elsewhere, but a compelling diplomacy capable of proposing and reaching an accommodation with Russia at least in Europe. It would be a final irony if NATO continued to weaken itself at the very historical moment when the Soviet empire is undergoing its greatest crisis, and when the Soviet system in the U.S.S.R. is facing a long-term breakdown.

The present Euromissile episode ought to be seen in this perspective: a test of the Alliance's will to resist and to defend itself, but also an opportunity to make peace—and on favorable terms.

Lawrence D. Freedman

U.S. Nuclear Weapons in Europe: Symbols, Strategy and Force Structure

Since the early 1950s there has rarely been a time when American nuclear weapons based in Europe have not been a source of controversy. The disagreements that have developed between the United States and Europe have covered a wide range of issues: the effects of the weapons on military tactics and the overall conduct of war; the nature of the threat they pose to the Soviet Union and the dividing line between deterrence and provocation; the extent to which it is proper for the European allies, particularly West Germany, to have control over these weapons and the form this control might take; and the degree to which the type of deployment has either helped to cement the Alliance or threatened to tear it asunder. The weapons themselves have come in all shapes and sizes—mines, artillery shells, gravity bombs, and a great variety of missiles. They have been named after great figures in American folklore (Davy Crockett), famous generals (Pershing), Norse gods (Thor), and weapons of an earlier age (Lance and Tomahawk). They have been under single U.S. control or as part of allied armed forces under some sort of dual-key arrangement.

The recent nuclear debate has been more intense and broadly based than those of the past. Nevertheless, it has only touched on a few of the issues associated with American weapons in Europe. Even though most of the important issues mentioned above have been raised at one time or another, especially in official circles, by and large the focus has been on the new intermediate-range nuclear forces (INFs) while the debate has been phrased in terms of the dangers of the nuclear arms race or the cohesion of NATO.

This debate may subside once the first group of missiles is firmly in place and operational. However, large-scale political movements may remain in a high state of mobilization throughout

Europe and with deployment not scheduled for completion until 1988, the debate may not diminish. At any rate, too many offical and unoffical studies and complex negotiations have been set in motion, and too many awkward questions raised, for the NATO establishment to let the matter rest. For the moment the INF question is being managed, but there will be plenty of opportunity for renewed controversy in the future. Some in the protest movements would argue that even if governments wished the nuclear issue to go away, leaving in its wake the flotsam of exhausted editorialists, publishers, and producers of TV documentaries, the danger of the course upon which we are now embarked will force the issue back onto the agenda.

By contrast the NATO establishment is preparing to breathe a collective sigh of relief. The great danger of a successful Soviet exploitation of Alliance confusion and dissension appears to have been averted. The urgency has been taken out of the issue. Any stocktaking may extend no further than looking back to see how public opinion can be "handled" more effectively in the future. I will touch on this matter briefly toward the end of this essay. My main concern, however, is with the structure of NATO's nuclear arsenal. The debate that has developed has revealed an understandable amount of confusion, even among NATO loyalists, as to what the basic rationales underlying nuclear policy are or should be. This essay attempts to deal with this problem by first, describing the rationales, and then, discussing the kind of force structure that might most effectively reflect these rationales. Finally, the essay will address this issue in the context of both arms control and Alliance defense policy.

It is my contention that a number of developments may be in train which together represent a sensible adjustment in NATO nuclear policy. Progress up to now has been somewhat fortuitous and the logic of the changes in policy has yet to be fully worked out. This process of adjustment has been helped neither by the unconvincing and often self-contradictory rationales used to justify particular deployments nor by the excessive symbolism surrounding the whole nuclear issue. In order to understand and encourage these developments, it will be necessary to return to first principles and from there construct a case for a particular sort of U.S. nuclear deployment in Europe.

The Policy Shift

Before examining the basic principles of NATO doctrine, it might be useful to establish that a shift in policy is under way. NATO has provided few clues as to the nature of the evolution of its policy. The proposed introduction of cruise missiles and Pershing IIs was offically explained and justified by NATO officials in terms of continuity. This was evident in the 1979 NATO plan to replace 108 Pershing I missiles with the exact same number of Pershing IIs, and in the removal of the appropriate number of old nuclear warheads to make way for the arrival of new warheads with new missiles. It was reinforced in the language NATO leaders used to outline the plan that was described early on as an "evolutionary upward adjustment." Sounding much like bureaucratese for an extra turn of the screw, this term understandably never caught on. However, the more successful term adopted by NATO planners was "modernization," and it has stuck. This claim to be doing little more than improving a well-established capability has been emphasized in any number of placatory official NATO statements since 1979.

How warranted is this impression of continuity? Certainly there have been American nuclear weapons in Europe since the 1950s. The issue for NATO nuclear planners throughout the 1970s was how this early generation should be replaced. It would have been surprising if the new generation had been less capable than its predecessor. To use an overworked analogy, one expects when buying a new car to have improved steering, fuel consumption, reliability, and carrying capacity, and so it is with missiles. However, if one trades a family sedan for an Aston Martin, one is engaging in something more than modernization. The essential point about the move from Pershing I to Pershing II is not increased accuracy or speed, but the fact that the new missile can hit Soviet territory, whereas the old one could not.

It can be argued that there are precedents for such a capability. In the late 1950s and the early 1960s the Thor and Jupiter intermediate-range missiles were based in Great Britain, Italy and Turkey and were capable of reaching the Soviet Union; then for much of the 1960s the Mace cruise missile was based in West Germany. The point is that the removal of these missiles was not the result of age but a deliberate political choice *not* to have missiles of such range based in Europe.

During the 1970s a European-based threat to Soviet territory was sustained by offshore U.S. Poseidon submarines, but the American link to Europe was made somewhat tenuous by the unavoidable fact that submarines have an enviable capacity for turning around and going home should it be decided that their previous commitment was unwise. The counting of Poseidon in the Strategic Arms Limitation Treaty (SALT) negotiations, moreover, created a closer association of the Poseidons with the central U.S.-Soviet strategic balance than with the European theater. The remaining systems actually based in Europe were long-range aircraft, such as the American F-111 or the British Vulcan. There was always uncertainty as to whether these aircraft could penetrate air defenses, and some of them were required for other, more pressing, conventional purposes. Now, the British Vulcans have been withdrawn. In short, it is clear upon reexamination of the composition of NATO's nuclear arsenal over the last 25 years that to install new land-based missiles capable of hitting the Soviet Union at this point is more than modernization—it reflects an important shift of policy.

The soothing language of "stability" and "modernization" used by Western leaders along with their encouraging references to arms control would, it was hoped, hide this shift and take the steam out of the anticipated opposition. The nature of the likely opposition had been seen a couple of years earlier with the dispute over the enhanced radiation weapon, more popularly known as the neutron bomb.

The political debate—indeed, passion—over this issue could not be kept in check. NATO's 1979 dual-track decision to deploy cruise missiles and Pershing IIs in Europe while simultaneously pursuing arms control negotiations was immediately followed by the dramatic deterioration in the international situation that ensued from the Soviet invasion of Afghanistan and led to the demise of the SALT II Treaty. The modernization effort appeared as part of a more general East-West confrontation and acquired quite sinister connotations. Far from being the latest stage in a long-established practice of maintaining and refurbishing a nuclear arsenal that happened to be based in Europe, the introduction of the missiles was seen by the rapidly growing protest groups to be a dangerous new act of escalation; it was part of America's private battle with the Soviet Union—except only Europe was likely to suffer the consequences. The protesters believed that behind the NATO decision there was an American plot designed to facilitate the waging of a limited nuclear war or, alternatively (and in contradiction), to inflict a surprise first strike on the Soviet Union. Even many who accepted the deployment decision as being based on a deterrence rationale assumed that the effort was brought about largely at American instigation and in pursuit of a peculiarly American concept of nuclear strategy.

This is not the place to trace the history of NATO's December 1979 decision. It is reasonably clear from the record that the main impetus came from Europe rather than the United States. More important, the decision went against what had been a pronounced inclination in American policy to oppose the basing of intermediate-range missiles in Europe. The prominence of the American position in NATO, the facts that the decision was in favor of American missiles under American control and that the most strident opponents were European, obscured the essential significance of what had taken place: at a time of comparative weakness in the American position vis-à-vis its allies, the United States had agreed to increase its nuclear exposure in Europe.

The American weakness was largely a result of the neutron bomb debacle. In April 1978, with the ground prepared for a production decision, President Carter drew back from this step. European leaders who had, without enthusiasm, agreed to incur whatever political costs the arrival of this weapon entailed, were embarrassed and irritated at being left looking foolish by this last-minute reversal of policy. The decision to press ahead with intermediate-range nuclear forces was taken partly as a result of the neutron bomb incident in an effort to demonstrate that NATO in general, and the United States in particular, could still take and implement awkward nuclear decisions.

The irony was that the enhanced radiation weapon, far more than cruise missiles or Pershing IIs, fitted in with American concepts for NATO nuclear strategy. Yet in the neutron bomb episode it was the Europeans who stood firm, at least relatively speaking, while the Americans wobbled. In the INF case Europe wavered while the Americans remained constant. Some in the Reagan Administration recognized that it was strange to be demanding that European governments stay true to a process which they had initiated but which could be seen as reducing U.S. control over its own nuclear destiny. Nevertheless, such thoughts were always overridden by the perceived necessity to see through a collective decision and not to give an inch to the protest movements.

The shift in NATO's nuclear posture represented by the failure to adopt the neutron bomb and the agreement to introduce intermediate-range nuclear forces may be carried through in other elements of NATO's nuclear posture. Recent studies in the High-Level Group of NATO on short-range or battlefield nuclear weapons may result in a general reduction. The nature of the shift can be illustrated by reference to the last time that there was a serious debate in NATO on the overall character of its nuclear stockpile.

During 1974-75, in response to a request from Senator Sam Nunn for a report on the subject, the U.S. Department of Defense had to sort out a rationale for the size and composition of its European-based nuclear forces. Reflecting European concerns that came to light during Alliance consultations, the Defense Department concluded that even though there might be no pressing military purposes served by maintaining a force at the then-current level, the number of warheads (7,000) deployed had assumed a symbolic significance such that any diminution would be taken to indicate a weakening in the U.S. nuclear guarantee to Europe. On the other hand, in the 1983 discussions, it has been the Europeans who have been pressing for a reduction in the overall nuclear stockpile, while the Americans have been arguing the need to maintain numbers for military purposes. Clearly, there is a shift in policy under way, but the question is whether it matters and therefore whether it should be encouraged or resisted. To answer this we need to get back to first principles.

Return to First Principles

The case for a U.S. nuclear arsenal in Europe does *not* depend on the two most common arguments put forward in its favor. The first states that so long as the Soviet Union maintains weapons in one or the other of the "theater" categories—that is, either intermediate or battlefield nuclear weapons of sufficient range to reach targets in Europe or Asia but insufficient to reach the United States—NATO must have available weapons in these same categories. This is a "force-matching" rationale. The second states that so long as NATO is inferior in its conventional forces, then it has no choice but to depend on the threat of nuclear first-use. This threat, the argument continues, can only be made credible by the presence of nuclear weapons liable to be caught up early in any continental battle.

The first argument makes only a case for the shorter range or battlefield theater nuclear weapons which might be able to strike targets of opportunity. This begs the question of their actual military utility, to which we will return presently. When it comes to attacking fixed targets inside the Soviet Union, all that needs to be launched can be launched well away from Western Europe. As the Warsaw Pact and NATO are quite different politically, geographically and militarily, there is no strategic argument for crude force-matching. The Soviet need for a distinct class of intermediate-range nuclear forces could be said to follow from the wide geographical spread of its potential enemies. Despite its logical flaws, force-matching seems to satisfy some deep psycho-political need not to allow any "gaps" to develop. However, since there are financial and structural limits to NATO's ability to meet this need, it is unwise to pander to the force-matching notion at all.

The trouble with the second argument is that it encourages the notion that if only the West could pull itself together and achieve a sufficient conventional deterrent, there would then be no need for U.S. nuclear weapons in Europe. If NATO could improve its conventional capability, and again this is a matter to which we will return, then it certainly could reduce the strategic demands placed on the nuclear force; but even if the purpose is no more than to threaten retaliation against a Soviet nuclear attack, then some nuclear capability is still needed.

The real case for U.S. nuclear weapons in Europe is that they provide the best available, though by no means perfect, answer to the problems posed to Western Europe by sharing a continent with a nuclear superpower.

It is hoped by some that a transformation of European politics might remove the security problem altogether. The proposition is put forward by the European anti-nuclear protest movements that if only the European members of NATO and the Warsaw Pact could free themselves from their superpower masters, then they could come together with a renewed sense of their common culture and destiny.

The political objections to this are profound. There is an essential unreality in assuming that the East European position is at all analogous to the Western position, let alone that the East can liberate itself from the Soviet thrall without frightening and dangerous convulsions. Even if this could be achieved successfully, there is no reason to believe that all would be sweetness and light. It is hardly the case that prior to American and Soviet intrusion, Europe was one big happy family. Nor would it necessarily be the case, following the dissolution of the existing alliances, that individual states would not turn to external sources for security purposes. Under any conceivable circumstances, Soviet nuclear power is going to be overbearing. The problem is therefore long term; it is either to be vulernable to Soviet nuclear pressure or to have some means of resisting such pressure.

For West Europeans there are three alternative ways of dealing with Soviet nuclear pressure. The first is to accede to it and accept the resulting Soviet influence over their affairs. The second is to counter it by developing a national capacity for nuclear retaliation. The third is to draw on the deterrent effect of another nuclear power.

All of the NATO countries have rejected the first option. France and the United Kingdom have decided to rely on nuclear capabilities under national control to resist Soviet pressure. The remainder depend on the third option—a nuclear guarantee by another country. It is this dependence that has led to most of the perplexing dilemmas related to nuclear deterrence. These dilemmas stem from inevitable doubts on the part of the guarantor country as to whether it is wise to attempt to extend deterrence in this manner, and from worries on the part of the guaranteed countries as to whether deterrence will, in practice, be extended.

It might have been thought that the most obvious source of a nuclear guarantee for the non-nuclear West European nations would be Great Britain and France. But the requirement existed and the commitments were made well before the British and French deterrents were constructed. These deterrents were designed for national purposes only. This is absolutely clear in the French case and reasonably so in the British case. Great Britain has assigned its nuclear force to NATO (as required by the 1962 Nassau Agreement). In private the commitment is less firm. It is almost impossible to find a statement by a senior British politician out of office that assumes that the purpose of the national force is anything other than a "last resort" deterrent for Britain. It has increasingly been portrayed in this way by those in office: they have called the British nuclear force the "ultimate guarantor of our national security."

Great Britain has accepted a degree of nuclear exposure in West Germany and, with France, it claims to add to NATO's overall deterrent through the uncertainty induced in the Soviet mind by the existence of three nuclear decision centers. However, any contribution to the nuclear protection of the allies is not self-sufficient—it only makes sense in the context of a U.S. nuclear guarantee. The uncertainty generated in the Soviet mind by London and Paris is quite marginal compared with that generated by Washington. In a conflict the British and French forces would seem to be a manageable problem for the U.S.S.R. as long as Moscow was prepared to grant these two nations the sanctuary status that their nuclear forces are really designed to secure.

Oddly enough, the person who has most pushed to the fore the possibility of a European deterrent based on Anglo-French nuclear forces is Soviet President Yuri Andropov. His proposal in the INF talks calling for the withdrawal of all U.S. nuclear-equipped aircraft and opposing the deployment of new U.S. missiles, while linking the number of SS-20 warheads to those on British and French missiles, assigns a far greater responsibility to those European missiles than their owners have ever claimed.

In this context, the West Germans have made clear once again that they would not exchange the U.S. guarantee for one from Great Britain and France. At best the Anglo-French forces are seen as the rudiments of some future European deterrent. For some European dreamers this would be the nucleus of a united and independent community. Others see it as no more than a second-best solution after an American withdrawal; this is how the British and French see their nuclear capabilities. However, they have really only taken out the insurance policy for themselves—and not for their neighbors.

A European deterrent of any sort would soon have to face the issue of the extent and nature of West German control. If the West Germans are not allowed to have their own "bomb," then some collaborative venture is required, complete with multiple manning and multiple vetoes. This would undoubtedly turn out to be as impractical as previous NATO-wide schemes of similar inspiration. Either the new force would have to be separate from the existing British and French forces, or else the two countries would have to cede sovereignty over their nuclear weapons. None of this seems likely.

Alternatively there could be a German bomb. In pure strategic terms this might appear as a simple and elegant solution to all of NATO's problems. At the heart of NATO's difficulty is the effective defense of West Germany. It is generally accepted that to threaten retaliation following an attack against one's own territory is about as credible as you can get with nuclear deterrence. Ergo, let West Germany develop its own nuclear deterrent. However, neither West Germany's neighbors nor the West Germans themselves have demonstrated any serious interest in this option. With so many vivid memories of past conventional offensives launched from German soil, there are still definite advantages in having West Germany dependent on others for its security.

If it is preferable that West Germany not "go nuclear" and if the British and French are unable or unwilling to provide a nuclear guarantee to West Germany and other non-nuclear allies, then the only alternative is that these countries continue to rely on the United States. If the Americans had known then what they know now, they might not have made a commitment to the nuclear protection of Europe in the first place. But the commitment was made when circumstances were more propitious, and to its credit the United States has not tried to take advantage of changes in the strategic environment to withdraw. The continuity of this nuclear alliance has become one of its greatest strengths. Establishing a new arrangement raises difficult questions as to motives and implications. Carrying on with the status quo avoids such questions.

So central is the U.S. nuclear guarantee that much time in

NATO is spent worrying about its durability. The reasons are familiar. The Soviet Union has the capacity to assure a devastating nuclear strike against American territory and therefore the Americans are unlikely to want to risk such a strike unless their supreme national interests are already very much in jeopardy. If some meaningful superiority could be established over the U.S.S.R., then the problem would be easier; but as this is not in the cards, the Europeans have to hope that the Americans will continue to view the maintenance of cooperative democratic governments in Western Europe and the prevention of Soviet domination of the whole continent as a supreme national interest.

Since there do not seem to be any preferable alternatives, the Europeans have little choice but to continue with an act of faith. Some Americans worry that European countries—and again they have West Germany most in mind—might become so alarmed at the incredibility of the U.S. guarantee that they would succumb readily to Soviet pressure and influence. This view tends to be based on exaggerated interpretations of continued West German interest in détente. NATO's proposed military remedies, which were designed to recover superiority, threaten to emphasize rather than ease West German anxieties about preventing the complete breakdown of East-West relations.

Most of the worrying about the U.S. nuclear guarantee, however, goes on in the United States rather than in Europe; but these anxieties normally focus on how to improve the guarantee rather than on how to get out of it. There is a constant need in Europe for the United States to provide frequent reassurance to the Europeans that their act of faith is warranted. Because the objective is to maintain existing security arrangements, the essential reassurance the Europeans have required is that the United States keep the situation as it is and avoid reappraisals of basic commitments or even hints of such.

NATO's Nuclear Symbols

To understand this need for reassurance it is necessary to acknowledge the role played by symbols in international politics. Long-term intentions are conveyed not only through appropriate diplomatic language but also through actions which signify the nature and extent of commitments. There is a great advantage in being able to convey potentially complex political messages in a simplified form that can be readily understood by all concerned. The whole concept of deterrence depends on the ability to insert a sense of risk into the minds of possible adversaries, and this requires a stark and uncomplicated form of presentation. So does a nuclear guarantee to allies. Neither message can risk being lost in the general noise of international communication or through an excess of subtlety.

Reliance on a policy of deterrence encourages a tendency toward symbolism, especially when the assumptions upon which the policy is based cannot be easily proved or disproved. Since the Soviet Union has not launched an attack on NATO, the natural presumption is that the Alliance is doing something right, and therefore it would be unwise to tamper with the policy of deterrence. This tendency is reinforced by the inertia that is a natural consequence of alliance. In NATO the capacity to adapt has become stifled by the sheer difficulty of obtaining agreement among a diverse collection of nations on a proper direction for change. Offical life becomes easier when it is possible to follow orthodoxy. The most prominent features of established policy and practice become shrouded in symbolism. What had once been fresh and controversial becomes incantation; spontaneity gives way to ritual.

The problem created by too much symbolism is that it inhibits thought and adaptation to changed circumstances. The symbols are sustained for their own sake without any assurance that the message they are supposed to impart remains valid, or that their meaning is at all evident to those who do not appreciate this form of communication. Rather than crude but effective ways of conveying fundamental messages, they become a form of code that requires interpretation by trained specialists, a phenomenon that can be recognized in the endless debate on Alliance strategy.

The U.S. commitment to European security is the sort of essential feature of international life that can be usefully underlined by symbolic action. But this is not true of relations at a less elevated level. Symbols are rarely suitable for fine-tuning relationships. Therefore, when the attempt is made to fine-tune them, confusion is likely to result.

If every aspect of Alliance security arrangements is taken to be politically significant, then deep political meaning will be read into any change. Yet often when change is initiated, some functional purpose is served as well as a higher symbolism. Thus, even if change had been deemed necessary for quite mundane reasons, it can trigger some quite disproportionate political reaction among those whose settled image of the order of things has been suddenly disturbed.

This latter point is important because the symbolism currently associated with U.S. nuclear weapons in Europe does not reflect the original purposes for which the weapons were introduced. "Tactical nuclear weapons" (as they were then called) were introduced into Europe in the early 1950s. At the time it seemed little more than a natural extension of the military exploitation of nuclear energy, which might even, some hoped, reduce dependence on strategies and weapons of mass destruction. Soon after, more destructive missiles and bombers were introduced to ensure that a severe U.S. nuclear threat to the Soviet Union could be sustained while intercontinental forces were under development. It was only later, when the Americans had no obvious need themselves for European bases and the Soviet Union was well on its way to achieving strategic parity, that the Europeans began to see the U.S. nuclear arsenal in Europe in essentially symbolic terms.

A rather passive approach calling for the United States to freeze its theater nuclear stockpile as an act of faith was reinforced by two factors: the failure in the early 1960s of more active policies, such as the ill-fated proposal for a Multilateral Nuclear Force (MLF) that was designed to give the Europeans a greater sense of nuclear responsibility; and the emergence in the late 1960s of a substantial body of opinion in Washington that advocated the reduction of the NATO commitment. Thus, for a while, a stockpile of 7,000 nuclear warheads was seen to be so essential that any reduction would lead to a commensurate loss in the cohesion of the Alliance.

Coexisting with this higher symbolism was a succession of military rationales. In the absence of any clear political criteria other than the maintenance of established numbers, purely military considerations tended to govern the nature and composition of the arsenal. This might have introduced a certain amount of order were it not for the unsatisfactory and inconsistent nature of

NATO's military plans. What has been lacking is a doctrine that links the NATO arsenal's military form to its political purpose.

Thus, as the early weapons became obsolete, and as the time came to introduce new systems, the process of modernization came to be governed by the deeper political meanings that had become attached to certain features of the force. New technological and tactical concepts had to be matched with entrenched political concepts. The attempt to achieve this began in the 1970s and at first proceeded smoothly. The Europeans agreed to let the Americans bring in whatever weapons they liked so long as the warhead stockpile was held firm. But this agnostic attitude toward technology and tactics in Europe meant that there was a lack of convincing rationale for the developing composition of the arsenal. Once the issue had been pushed to the fore with the "neutron bomb" controversy, the Europeans in particular were forced to address the issue in functional terms.

This task was further complicated by the development of a series of intra-Alliance debates which in themselves had only a slight military content, but which soon provided the context for the debate on the shape of the U.S. nuclear arsenal in Europe. In NATO argot the essential security link between North America and Western Europe is described as "coupling." This is what the symbolism is all about. A requirement for any new policy must be that it reinforces this coupling. The trouble has been that in a comparatively dynamic political situation the requirements for coupling are uncertain.

Coupling refers to the link between the defense of Europe and the U.S. nuclear arsenal. The basic point for all concerned is that there be such a link; and basing both U.S. nuclear and conventional forces in Europe underlines this point. However, the link is not created by the U.S. presence in Europe but by the American judgment that supreme national interests would be at stake if the Soviet Union were to extend its influence on the continent. "Decoupling" would result if policymakers in Washington no longer made the same judgment. But this would not be based on any determination that the nuclear force structure is badly designed.

Also, decoupling could occur if a significant portion of European opinion came to doubt that it wanted to be coupled with the United States. This is happening to some extent with the European protest movements. In these circumstances the symbols of the U.S. commitment have taken on a quite different meaning from that which had been intended. The same military forces that reassure one group can appear quite sinister to another with a less generous appreciation of American motives. If one attempts to satisfy both groups by fixing on a mutually acceptable form to the arsenal, then the symbolism is likely to get extremely confused, while the real anxieties are not addressed. Arguments in NATO during the early 1980s had little to do with the structure of the nuclear arsenal, and much more to do with foreign policy disagreements concerning the Soviet Union, the Middle East, and so on.

Moreover, the force structure that had developed by the late 1970s and early 1980s was quite complex and could not be easily fashioned according to subtle political requirements. Nevertheless, such an attempt was made in the December 1979 decision on intermediate-range nuclear forces. Some new systems were necessary to underline the U.S. commitment to Europe, but not so many as to suggest that a war might be conducted solely from Western Europe without involving U.S.-based strategic forces, or as to legitimize the concept of a "Euro-strategic balance." NATO did not want to give the impression that a Soviet "theater" attack would be dealt with on a separate European level rather than by involving the totality of U.S. nuclear power. For their part, the West Germans wanted other non-nuclear countries to host cruise missiles (the "non-singularity" condition) and wanted a single-key arrangement so that the West German position would not be given undue prominence. Later on, the capacity of the European host countries to implement the decision was perceived in Washington to be symbolic of the European readiness to accept its share of the risks and responsibilities of NATO membership.

However much this may have been appreciated by the *cognoscenti*, it was lost on the wider audience that was developing an interest in why these new weapons were to be introduced. In the public debate more basic prejudices and intuitive responses soon came to the fore, and politicians jettisoned the NATO orthodoxy with remarkable speed in order to save the program. The classic example of this was the adoption in November 1981 of the "zero option" for the Geneva negotiations. The idea in December 1979 had been that NATO had a unique requirement for intermediate-range nuclear forces, which was related to its own strategic circumstances and could not be explained by reference to Soviet weapons of comparable range. Yet two years later cruise missiles and Pershing IIs were presented as simple responses to the Soviet SS-20; and it was stated that if the SS-20 were to disappear, then so would the NATO requirement.

Indeed, the arms control negotiations themselves have provided further illustration of the tendency toward creeping symbolism. The Europeans have never fully developed criteria for judging the content of arms control proposals, even when they have been directly affected. Their interest has been in looking for signs of larger political movements. Thus in the early 1970s some Europeans suspected that SALT was the prelude to some superpower deal that could only come about at the expense of Europe's interests. Likewise, a decade later, proposals that Europeans would once have considered highly suspect were enthusiastically endorsed in order to sustain the spectacle of negotiating and demonstrate a capacity for East-West dialogue. In part this was a response to those in the United States who had attacked SALT, not so much for its output, but as a symbol of détente. Here again there was a tension between the symbolism and the ostensible purpose of the effort. Were individual proposals to be judged in terms of some functional criteria or in terms of a larger political game?

It is no part of my argument that a wholly clinical approach to the construction of NATO's nuclear posture should be adopted. Political insensitivity has been a common failing in contemporary strategic studies. It is important to recognize the larger strategic purposes that others believe are implied in measures taken for what were presumed to be reasonably innocuous technical reasons. Nor can one ignore the "placebo effect," which posits that if someone believes that something is doing him good, then it does do him good. Much of what is done in the name of deterrence in the West comes into this category.

The relationships among the NATO countries ought now to be sufficiently mature to make it possible for them to discuss their suspicions and reveal their innermost fears directly. It should not be necessary to work through coded messages or to lump together a variety of collective programs in order to satisfy a complex symbolism. Past symbolism has been retained because the Alliance has failed to develop a coherent and consistent set of criteria with which to assess the force structure. Therefore, the first step toward freeing NATO from excessive symbolism must be to develop such criteria.

Criteria for Intermediate-Range Nuclear Forces in Europe

The first question to ask is whether any basing of U.S. forces in Europe serves a functional purpose. The United States does not need a European base in order to launch an attack on the Warsaw Pact. Moreover, while it is a common presumption that a local nuclear force would be more responsive to European conditions and requirements, there is no reason in logic why this should be so, given that the ultimate control over the use of this force will remain with the president in Washington and that the consequences of any use will continue to be horrific for the American people. The decision to launch a punitive strike on Europe's behalf will not be made less agonizing by having the weapons placed so close to the scene of the crime.

But we are not trying to predict the course of a war; we are only considering the requirements of deterrence. Nuclear deterrence rests, not upon proven fact or concrete experience, but on a series of hunches and suspicions about calculations of risks and interests, costs and gains, of a very fundamental sort. There are no margins of error. It is very difficult to explain why *any* decision to use nuclear weapons can be rational—even after the enemy's first strike has landed—but potential aggressors dare not rely on such rationality. So long as a first strike cannot achieve full disarmament of the victim, then any aggressive action carries with it a risk of nuclear retaliation. Although the calculation of risk cannot be but subjective, certain assumptions are commonly made and have therefore become part of the strategic culture. It is felt that the risk is greatest if contemplating a nuclear attack on a nuclear power; smallest when considering a conventional attack on a non-nuclear, nonaligned power. In such deadly calculations geography does make a difference. Nuclear weapons based in Europe are more likely to get caught up in a conventional battle than those stationed safely out at sea, and this affects the likelihood of their use.

It does appear that the Soviet Union makes this assumption. Its strategic doctrine presupposes that a war will "go nuclear," though not that this is inevitable. What is envisioned is a conventional stage in which conditions are gradually made more suitable for a decisive nuclear strike. The strike will be undertaken, not as a desperate act of last resort, but as a deliberate move following successful conventional operations. The conventional phase is to be used to distribute nuclear weapons to the relevant units (all but a few warheads are kept safely in Soviet territory) and bring them to full combat readiness. At the same time Soviet conventional forces, including ground troops, would be seeking out and destroying the bulk of NATO's nuclear assets.

Such an approach has many problems. It makes it impossible to devote resources to a single-minded pursuit of a conventional victory and is crucially dependent on the design and timing of the nuclear strike. The right moment for the Soviets to initiate a nuclear strike would be when remaining NATO nuclear capabilities are susceptible to removal by a Soviet strike. This could be upset by a NATO move to use nuclear weapons first (in which case Soviet doctrine seems to require a highly unsatisfactory preemption), or simply by denying the Soviet Union the opportunity to destroy NATO's retaliatory capability in its strike. This, in turn, depends very much on whether or not U.S. "strategic" forces are going to be available to retaliate following a limited Soviet strike against Europe.

It must be emphasized that whatever the Soviet leaders say about the impossibility of "limited nuclear war" or the inevitability of escalation, their doctrine and plans, and indeed arms control proposals, only make sense if one assumes the possibility of Soviet territory being accepted as a sanctuary during nuclear hostilities. This can be seen in the Soviets' far greater concern about Pershing II (which can hit the U.S.S.R.), as opposed to Pershing I (which cannot); their preoccupations with "forward-based systems"; the holding of Soviet nuclear assets in Soviet territory, and so on. When Soviet commentators are attacking the notion of limited nuclear war, their target is not the protest movements' fear that exchanges will be confined to the superpowers' allies but the idea that the U.S.S.R. could be attacked from Western Europe with American nuclear weapons while American territory remained untouched. The hope would appear to be to convince the United

States that as long as Soviet territory is left alone, there will be no direct attack on U.S. territory, even though nuclear exchanges might be under way in the center of Europe.

Hence the Soviet concern about the cruise missiles and the Pershing IIs. These weapons introduce a European-based threat to the Soviet homeland that appears to be seen as distinct from and more dangerous than an American-based threat. The U.S.S.R. lacks defenses against these missiles (which is not the case with aircraft) and could only be sure of destroying them on the ground with a "bolt from the blue." Once the missile transporters have been moved out of base it would be difficult in practice to attack them successfully even with an area barrage.

The risk of retaliation against the Soviet homeland would still give the Kremlin pause for thought if the only threat were the central U.S. strategic forces. Nevertheless the location of the new NATO missiles dispels any Soviet illusions about containing the consequences of a nuclear strike in Central and Western Europe and as such performs a valuable function. There really does seem to be some substance to the idea that the physical presence of U.S. weapons on European soil not only provides reassurance to the Europeans but also significantly affects Soviet calculations.

The actual number of cruise missiles and Pershing IIs to be introduced depends on the course of the arms control negotiations, as well as the decisions by the host governments. The outcome is unlikely to be much less than 200 individual weapons, and this can be said to constitute NATO's minimum deterrent. The 400 Poseidon warheads assigned to the Supreme Allied Commander in Europe (the contents of two and a half submarines) provide an important complement because of their invulnerability. The fact that these appear in strategic arms control negotiations has created a concern that they will be double-counted in INF negotiations, and this has led to an unfortunate playing down of their European role.

Criteria for Battlefield Nuclear Weapons

Is there a need for anything other than these intermediate-range systems capable of attacking Soviet territory? I have not adduced that the essential military function of intermediate-range nuclear forces is related to defeating a Soviet conventional assault. The intention is to deny the Soviet Union nuclear options. It is a considerable bonus that the vulnerability of other key targets to nuclear attack, from air bases to troop concentrations to fuel dumps, will add to Soviet doubts as to their capacity to make good a conventional invasion. Unfortunately this contribution to the halting of a conventional attack is assumed to be the only one that matters for NATO. This erroneous impression has been nourished by the integration of NATO's other nuclear systems—gravity bombs, shells, depth charges, mines, short-range missiles, air-defense missiles, and so on—with its conventional forces.

The debate on whether these short-range nuclear weapons can be used on the battlefield to gain a decisive military advantage is almost as old as the Alliance itself. After the first rush of enthusiasm in the 1950s, which brought with it the first rush of weapons, two very large problems began to assert themselves. First, any use in sufficient numbers to achieve the required effect would result in massive death and destruction in the surrounding area, afflicting those supposedly being defended. Second, whatever advantages might be gained in a NATO strike would be lost in a Warsaw Pact counterstrike. The result would be a super-efficent war of attrition in which victory (if it can be called that) would go to the side with the greatest reserves and staying power. This would not necessarily be NATO.

One way to alleviate these disadvantages would be to unleash a nuclear strike in the early stages of a war when the invading forces were still concentrated and on their own territory. However, the fact that large numbers of East German rather than West German civilians would suffer would be no great consolation and the consequences of a Soviet counterstrike would still be dire. Given the likelihood of rapid escalation in the scope and intensity of nuclear exchanges, there would be great reluctance to authorize the strike until less apocalyptical measures had been exhausted even though conditions thereafter would become increasingly unfavorable. Despite NATO's dependence on the threat of nuclear first-use, the natural desire to avoid premature or unwarranted use has led to such time-consuming and complicated release procedures as to reduce severely any possible military gains.

The possibility of more "tailored" nuclear munitions designed to minimize collateral damage (such as "enhanced radiation weapons," also known as neutron bombs) fails to escape the consequences of Soviet retaliation. Moreover, there is a certain unreality in many of the claims made in behalf of such munitions in terms of reducing the impact on the local population. In a confusing and sprawling battle over highly urbanized areas of Germany, the large numbers of weapons that would have to be unleashed would soon spread their damage widely, despite efforts that might have been made to concentrate the effects of individual weapons. Finally, even while NATO might prefer to wait before authorizing nuclear use, the vulnerability of the facilities for nuclear use and the proximity of many weapons to the border means that NATO's hand could be forced by the prospect of the loss of these vital capabilities.

Meanwhile the maintenance of a battlefield nuclear capability diverts resources away from conventional forces. The weapons themselves have to be produced and a large and expensive special infrastructure maintained to store and handle them in Europe and control their distribution and use. The aircraft and artillery pieces designed to deliver them are, by and large, dual-capable, but the prospect of having to "go nuclear" means that a number of these delivery vehicles may have to be held back at a critical time rather than be committed to the immediate conventional battle.

Thus, preparation for battlefield nuclear use may make it more likely that non-nuclear methods will fail, while nuclear methods offer little hope for a favorable change in the course of a land battle. The only hope for success would be if the enemy did not respond to a nuclear strike in kind—a thin reed upon which to rely. However, it can be argued that the purpose of battlefield nuclear weapons is deterrence rather than war-fighting. Therefore might it not be that the presence of these weapons would serve as a formidable constraint on Soviet plans, even if we recognize they possess limited practical utility in the event that deterrence fails?

Soviet military plans do seem to be constrained in two ways. The risk of a nuclear strike by NATO forces the dispersal of Soviet capabilities so as not to provide overly tempting targets. It also requires, in the early stages of hostilities, a diversion of effort to knock out, where possible, NATO's nuclear assets. This task is made more difficult by the sheer number and variety of those assets.

The first of these constraints, however, is likely to remain even without the threat of attack from short-range nuclear weapons because of the threat posed by longer range systems and even the more advanced conventional systems. The second constraint might indeed be dissipated by the reduction of battlefield nuclear forces, but with it would also go the risk of NATO's nuclear hand being forced prematurely. Much of the Soviet naval effort might at one point have been dissipated in an effort to destroy Polaris SSBNs (nuclear-powered submarines carrying ballistic missiles). But the fact that the modern SSBNs are so invulnerable means that the Soviet Navy will occupy itself elsewhere, although most NATO officials would not consider this to be a net loss. Furthermore, of course, if nuclear assets were under attack by the Warsaw Pact, then NATO conventional forces would have to be diverted to protect them.

The next stage of the "deterrent" case for retaining battlefield nuclear weapons is to argue that their removal would mean increased reliance on conventional forces, which are just not up to the task. Even if a serious conventional deterrent were feasible, which is doubtful, it would not necessarily be desirable. If the U.S.S.R. were reasonably confident that a war would not escalate into a nuclear exchange, then it might well feel that it had an excellent chance of prevailing by using its superior conventional capabilities, and that even if it should fail, it would survive to fight another day. Germany, by contrast, would be left almost as wrecked and desolate as if it had been the victim of a nuclear attack.

Although this is not the place to go into the prospects of, or prerequisites for, an improved conventional deterrent, a few points are worth noting. First, it is common to assess conventional forces in terms of war-fighting rather than in terms of deterrence. This is mistaken. The requirement is that the Soviet leaders cannot be sure of victory, not that NATO must be sure of repelling a Soviet invasion. The many uncertainties connected with warfare under contemporary conditions—system reliability and operability, command and control, climate, morale, training and stamina—can be expected to play a large part in inducing caution in Soviet planners, even while they also complicate NATO plans. It would be unfortunate if substantial sources of deterrence were neglected because of programs that stipulate unreal and unnecessary standards for evaluating NATO's capability. This can only result in disappointment and disillusion. In practice, and taking into account the morale factor, it is likely that if a Warsaw Pact invasion of Western Europe were thwarted by NATO, momentum could quickly shift to the point where the Pact's defeat would be turned into a rout and the war soon taken into Eastern Europe.

Second, and partly because of the previous point, the consequences of failure for the Soviet system should not be underestimated. A defeat of any sort would probably lead to immense political convulsions within Eastern Europe and even in the Soviet Union itself. Third, if an actual fight is envisioned, battlefield nuclear weapons, for the reasons discussed above, cannot compensate for conventional deficiencies. Since it is as likely as not that nuclear release would not be authorized until the battle had already been lost, then the existence of battlefield nuclear weapons is not going to change the course of the conflict. It would be unwise for commanders to assume that vital targets would be dealt with by nuclear means.

In terms of deterrence, battlefield nuclear weapons do create the possibility that a drift into nuclear escalation might just occur as a result of decisions taken for ostensibly military purposes. Whatever increment to deterrence this provides, it would seem to be outweighed by the confusion that has been introduced into NATO strategy by three problems associated with battlefield nuclear weapons: the need to provide a rationale for these weapons; the diversion of resources from conventional forces for the production and maintenance of battlefield nuclear weapons; and should deterrence fail, the dangers they bring of premature escalation into nuclear exchanges.

No-First-Use

From this discussion two roles emerge for U.S. nuclear forces in Europe. The first and most basic is to threaten strategic retaliation—that is against the centers, or at least vital assets, of the Soviet state—in the event of a Soviet nuclear strike against Western Europe. This would undermine the Soviet strategy for nuclear operations within Europe.

The second role, for which forces capable of hitting the Soviet heartland are not required, is to provide the prospect of escalation.

That is, a route to all-out nuclear war is suggested that in addition offers the possibility of stopping along the way before the disaster is complete. This capability is also needed in order to provide a less-than-total response to Soviet limited use. It has been argued that the prospect of escalation should not be created by integrating battlefield nuclear weapons with conventional forces. In practice it is likely that any impulse toward first-use of nuclear weapons in the West would be punitive, born of fear and anger at a Soviet invasion. Such an act of desperation is always possible, even if unlikely, and this possibility provides another marginal increment to deterrence. It does not require a large number of weapons. Although targets could be chosen in the hope of impeding a Soviet advance, the purpose of nuclear use must be retributive. It is a punishment for sustained aggression.

Both roles are consistent with a clear policy decision not to resort to early nuclear use in an attempt to prevail in a land war. This has already been implicitly agreed upon in the establishment of consultative and release procedures that would make early use extremely difficult to organize even if it were deemed desirable.

A promise not to use nuclear weapons first is unrealistic. We cannot know what will happen during a fierce and bloodly conflict. It would be no service to peace and stability for the superpowers to be able to move to war in the expectation that hostilities would remain non-nuclear. An image of the holocaust must never be allowed to slip from the minds of our statesmen. What does make sense is for NATO to plan its military operations on the presumption that nuclear forces will not be used and should not be needed. The extent to which a sufficient conventional deterrent can be put together, which is a matter of degree not of absolutes, is beyond the scope of this essay. What has been argued is that the case for the use of nuclear weapons for battlefield purposes fails on its own account and cannot be revived by pointing to problems of a different sort in the conventional sphere.

Policy Recommendations for , NATO's Nuclear Force Structure

Several conclusions flow from this analysis:

1) It is important that NATO proceeds with its INF program. Some deployment will be necessary even in the unlikely event that

the U.S.S.R. withdraws all its intermediate-range forces. Poseidon submarine-launched ballistic missiles should continue to be assigned to NATO as a survivable resource force, and more publicity should be given to this role.

2) Dual-purpose short-range weapons should be reorganized for dedicated conventional use. Any other dual-purpose weapons of greater range should be dedicated to nuclear use. Although it is of a shorter range than is really desirable, and does have some conventional capability, the Lance missile might come into this latter category. So might the Pershing I, which will soon be held only by West German forces on a dual-key basis. It would probably make sense for a new mobile missile—a true successor to the Pershing I—to be developed for European deployment. A development of this sort would only be tolerable politically in the context of substantial reductions, and possibly total elimination, of other battlefield nuclear weapons. The troops accompanying these weapons and the supporting infrastructure should be quite distinct from those used for conventional forces. A more clearly defined nuclear force structure may offer a simpler set of targets for a local Soviet first strike, but there would still be sufficient numbers and variety to make this difficult. The problem could be further mitigated by keeping the bulk of NATO's nuclear capability well away from the front line. I have not discussed the so-called defensive weapons—Nike-Hercules air-defense missiles and the atomic demolition munitions. These are relics of a bygone age for which there is now no rationale. They should be removed at once.

3) NATO should *not* make a no-first-use declaration but could make a clear statement of intent to rely on conventional forces in the event of war. In doing so, the particular horrors, risks and uncertainties of conventional war should be emphasized. Their deterrent value tends to get disregarded in the stress on the even greater evils of nuclear war.

4) NATO should significantly and unilaterally reduce its battlefield nuclear weapons; this is the most basic change needed. To understand the rationale for this we have to recognize the important shift that is taking place as a result of the introduction of the intermediate-range nuclear forces in Europe. This in turn requires consideration of why it is that the existing force structure varies so markedly from the guidelines outlined in the previous section. The answer in part is that this structure reflects past assumptions

and expectations, military rationales, and technical developments. Another crucial influence has been an American predisposition that can be characterized as follows: We would prefer not to have nuclear weapons in Europe because we fear that this will be a powder trail to a general conflagration. Furthermore, if nuclear weapons are to be deployed then we would prefer them to be shorter rather than longer range in the hope that a firebreak could be established so that any nuclear exchange might be contained in Europe. And if these weapons are to be integrated with U.S. air and ground forces, then they should at least be related to military needs and draw upon the latest technical advances.

European concerns have been so bound up with ensuring some U.S. nuclear presence that the Europeans have too readily yielded to the American preference for short-range systems designed for battlefield use. The Europeans want to emphasize the "strategic" purposes of the nuclear arsenal, in the sense of a decisive threat to the Soviet Union, rather than stress the "tactical" purposes of the arsenal, in the sense of its restricted threat to Soviet battlefield objectives.

There is now no need to get lost in the classic contrast of perceptions where Europeans fear a limited war fought by the superpowers all over their territory, while Americans suspect the Europeans of attempting to organize matters so that a local conflict will immediately escalate to the point where the superpowers exchange nuclear strikes safely over European heads. With the INF program under way, the United States has confirmed both its commitment to the nuclear defense of Europe and accepted that it will have intermediate-range systems on European soil. This means that the possibility of establishing a firebreak after short-range nuclear use has been dramatically undermined. This changes the context in which the short-range systems should be viewed in Washington. It is now as much in the American as in the European interest to reduce the chances of an early nuclear entanglement.

The wrench will be in acknowledging that the substantial NATO nuclear arsenal has slight military value, as traditionally conceived, and that it should be drastically cut and reorganized in order to give priority to its vital deterrent function. This is not going to be easy for many in the armed services of the allied countries, and since it involves a unilateral reduction of forces, it goes against the grain of East-West relations. The success of the proposal therefore depends on the coherence of the central strategic concept and the conviction with which it is held.

This approach does not involve, nor should it be made contingent upon, the success of arms control negotiations. NATO's force structure should reflect its own priorities and strategic concept and not those of the Soviet Union. If unilateral reductions allow for a more coherent force structure, then they should be implemented whether or not the U.S.S.R. wishes to follow suit. Furthermore, everything we know about the nature of arms control negotiations suggests that it would be very unwise to enter into yet another round of arms control discussions, this time on short-range nuclear systems. These arsenals defy categorization, comparison and verification. Therefore talks focusing exclusively on short-range, battlefield weapons might combine the worst features of the MBFR (mutual and balanced force reduction) and INF negotiations. If NATO cuts its short-range forces, it should naturally ask the U.S.S.R. to follow suit, but it should be neither dismayed nor surprised if little happens.

Policy Recommendations for Arms Control

Within the INF talks, arms control should also have the subordinate role, though here, of course, one cannot ignore the political stakes now bound up with the success or failure of the negotiations. The argument on the functional purpose served by intermediate-range nuclear forces as set out earlier does provide some criteria for assessing arms control proposals in this area:

1) Some intermediate-range missiles capable of hitting Soviet territory from Western Europe are necessary. The zero option, let alone a "zero-plus option," should remain jettisoned because of its flawed strategic logic as much as its lack of negotiability.

2) The essential feature of the INF deployment is the link that intermediate-range nuclear forces provide between the central strategic balance and a land war in Europe. They are not intended to provide a nuclear means of turning a land war in NATO's favor if deterrence fails, but they are meant to provide a prospect of escalation to help ensure that deterrence does not fail. Separate INF talks lose this essential point by attenuating the link with the

central strategic forces, and they confuse the issue by encouraging comparisons with Soviet forces of equivalent range. The separation of INF negotiations from strategic arms reduction talks (START) was a historical accident, the result of the peculiar political circumstances of 1980 and 1981. At the earliest possible opportunity the two sets of talks should be reintegrated.

3) The British and French forces do not and could not deter a Soviet nuclear attack on West Germany and there is no justification for Soviet formulas which balance SS-20s against the British and French missiles. This does not mean that there is *no* basis for Soviet concern. The Kremlin has a point in complaining that if all Soviet forces are to be constrained, then so should those of all its potential enemies. One method would be through a trade in the interstices of some merged INF-START negotiation. The problem here is that implicit credit was given the U.S.S.R. for the British and French forces in 1972 in SALT I, and that has not stopped the Soviets from coming back for something more explicit. Since an explicit credit would be difficult to reconcile with the expectations of the U.S. Congress regarding U.S.-Soviet parity, the best approach might be direct bilateral deals between Moscow and London and Paris.

4) Since the number of SS-20s deployed does not matter enormously, once a certain level has been passed, there should be no worry about accepting slightly larger Soviet numbers as long as the legitimacy of some NATO deployments have been accepted. Moreover, if all that NATO has to sweeten the pill for the Kremlin is the abandonment of the Pershing program, then this should be put forward. The strategic purposes can be adequately met by cruise missiles. On the other hand, NATO could not accept any outcome that leaves the threat to Japan and other Pacific states unconstrained while the threat to Western Europe is limited.

We are now at the point in the arms control negotiations where the basic positions are well known and progress depends on concessions that can be granted only for political reasons. It does not seem profitable to attempt great tactical ingenuity in negotiations. Long-term arms control aims should be pursued along with force planning objectives if NATO can develop a clear idea of priorities.

My argument has been that with developed and consistent criteria for force planning we can avoid the confusion and the drift into symbolism that has characterized past discussions about U.S. nuclear weapons in Europe. The debate of the past few years has been cathartic and, by forcing matters back to first principles, has helped to expose the emptiness of the ingrained orthodoxies on deterrence.

Equally erroneous would be the conclusion that nuclear policy is so difficult that governments must be spared the burden of controversy in this area. First, it is important to recognize that much of the discontent in recent years has had much more to do with the sour state of East-West relations, and of international politics in general, than with the particular hardware that has served as the focal point for public passions. The best source of public reassurance is a calm and thoughtful diplomacy, not an avoidance of important issues.

Second, while the past few years may have been traumatic for high-level policymakers, a lesson can be drawn that is more comforting. It would be a shame if the NATO establishment concluded from recent experience that all that is necessary to cope with popular discontent is to stonewall in the firm belief that superior political clout will prevail in the end. For a start, the consolidation of NATO's position has come at the expense of the center-left of European politics. In part this was its own fault, born of an understandable nervousness about accepting the logic of what appeared to be a hard-line policy when the hard line was becoming suspect. Nevertheless, it would be unwise for the NATO establishment to relax and rely on the continued success of the right.

For a while governments and their publics have been forced to look behind the symbolism. It would be a shame if they now returned the symbolism to its former glory without at least making the effort to create something that could help establish a much more substantial basis for consensus in the Alliance. Furthermore, the political devices that worked well this time, such as the promise of energetic arms control activity, may have lost their appeal for the next time, especially if nothing of substance emerges from Geneva.

The reasons why, in the end, the December 1979 decision survived may reflect as much good luck as management, but to some measure it may be because the program could be justified in the cut and thrust of public debate. Here the SS-20 helped, but so did the erroneousness of much of the criticism, especially that relating to "limited nuclear war." If the neutron bomb rather than intermediate-range nuclear forces had been the subject of the December 1979 meeting, then there would have been much more trouble in the ensuing years.

The most important point is that the Alliance must not be tempted to use the recent debate as a case study of how to push through modernization but instead should see the debate as evidence of the need to sort out the rationale for NATO's nuclear force. This rationale can provide a compelling argument for basing intermediate-range U.S. nuclear weapons in Europe.

Paul C. Warnke

The Illusion of NATO's Nuclear Defense

The intense interest generated on both sides of the Atlantic by the deployment of intermediate-range American nuclear missiles in Western Europe highlights the persistence of a dangerous misconception. Both the supporters and the opponents have framed the debate largely in military terms. In so doing, they perpetuate the illusion that nuclear weaponry is somehow integral to the defense of Western Europe against Soviet attack. There persists the decades-old reluctance to face up to the fact that employment of nuclear weapons by NATO could under almost no conceivable circumstances contribute to a successful defense.

But missed opportunities and misconceptions about the military value of intermediate-range nuclear forces (INFs) have made it almost certain that such weapons will be deployed by NATO, that this will lead to further deployments by the Soviet Union and that both East and West will become less secure. What has previously been a sideshow in the strategic nuclear arms competition has become a major source of division within the NATO Alliance and of confrontation with the Warsaw Pact.

Beyond question, the Soviet Union bears the principal responsibility for precipitating this largely political crisis. It is of course true that prior to 1977, and the initial deployment of the Soviet SS-20 medium-range ballistic missile, the Soviet Union was able to devastate all of Western Europe with its SS-4 and SS-5 ballistic missiles of intermediate-range and with that portion of its SS-11 intercontinental ballistic missile force then targeted against NATO. Had the SS-20 deployment merely lived up to its billing by the Soviets as a replacement for the aging SS-4s and SS-5s, which are liquid fueled, hard to maintain, and not very accurate, the felt need for an American INF counterpart might not have arisen. But the number of SS-20s now is reported to be about 360. Each of the missiles has three warheads, and, because they are mounted on mobile launchers, the entire number has to be considered as potentially capable of striking West European targets. As a consequence, rather than the 600 to 700 warheads previously carried by Soviet intermediate-range missiles, the number is now about 1,200—lower in total tonnage but of far greater accuracy. Over 200 SS-4s and SS-5s remain operational.

The Soviet SS-20 deployment predictably gave rise to discomfort among our NATO allies. From the military standpoint, it was argued that something had to be done to restore what was called the "Euro-strategic balance"—a concept of highly debatable merit that appears to rest on an assumption that U.S. willingness to use nuclear weapons against Soviet targets will be significantly influenced by the range and launching point of such missiles. Less abstruse and more convincing was the argument that the lack of a NATO response could lead the Soviet Union to feel that the United States was more interested in protecting the environment for bilateral U.S.-Soviet arms control talks than in assuaging the fears of its allies.

But one notion achieved considerable currency: an increase in Soviet nuclear missiles able to strike NATO Europe but not the United States could only be offset by American missiles able to strike the Soviet Union from NATO Europe. Analytically, it suffers from the defect common to all contentions that particular categories of Soviet nuclear weapons must be matched system-for-system in order to preserve deterrence. This rationale, for example, is heavily relied upon by supporters of the MX intercontinental ballistic missile. Because the Soviets have a big lead in ICBM warheads and throw-weight, MX proponents insist that the United States must build up its own ICBM force. Despite the fact that the Soviet ICBM lead is more than compensated for by the wide American lead in submarine-launched ballistic missiles and strategic bombers now being equipped with long-range air-launched cruise missiles. The same preoccupation with countering Soviet systems rather than acquiring useful American forces exists outside the nuclear field. It has been argued successfully in support of binary nerve gas production, for example.

The fact that the considerations involved in the INF debate are overwhelmingly political rather than military can be seen by the modest scope of the pending U.S. deployment. There are no plans to equal the Soviets in total INF warheads. The 464 ground-launched cruise missiles and 108 Pershing II missiles can add nothing militarily significant to the ability to blow up Soviet and East European targets. All important military, industrial and urban facilities in the Warsaw Pact's geographic area are redundantly covered by the 10,000 warheads now carried on American intercontinental and submarine-launched ballistic missiles and strategic bombers.

Ironically, the major stimulus for the West European interest in these new American missiles came from exaggerated anticipations of the success of the talks between the United States and the Soviet Union on limiting the intercontinental-range forces. Western leaders, notably the then-Chancellor of the Federal Republic of Germany, Helmut Schmidt, were concerned that while the Strategic Arms Limitations Treaties (SALT) steadily reduced the Soviet threat to North America, Western Europe would become hostage to an increasing number of the new Soviet SS-20 intermediate-range missiles. Should this occur, our NATO allies understandably feared it would "decouple" American security from their own.

Deterrence: "In the Eye of the Beholder"

This would, of course, be avoided if both Soviet SS-20s and potential American nuclear warheads to be based in Europe were included in the SALT process. The Protocol to the SALT II treaty—permitting testing and development of ground- and sea-launched cruise missiles but barring deployment until after 1981—was intended to preserve the potential of these systems as bargaining leverage to bring about controls on and reductions of the Soviet SS-20s and the older SS-4s and SS-5s. Discussions in the North Atlantic Council in 1977 and 1978 ended with acceptance of the American position that the Protocol would not be a precedent for indefinite inhibition on U.S. INF and that the Protocol restrictions would not be extended in the absence of effective control of Soviet INF.

Against this backdrop, the NATO Ministers reached their "dual-track decision" in December of 1979. For most of them, as Helmut Schmidt has since affirmed, the preferred solution was an arms control agreement that would make European basing of

American missiles unnecessary. Indeed, the decision itself specifically called for prompt ratification of the SALT II treaty and inclusion of INF in the SALT III negotiations. The United States has not met either of these requirements.

At the same time, however, there existed and still exists a strain of strategic thinking that elevates these U.S. intermediate-range nuclear missiles to a separate status of deterrent efficacy. For example, Foreign Minister Claude Cheysson of France has questioned even the "zero-zero option"—the initial American proposal under which the new American missiles would not be deployed if the Soviet Union scrapped its total intermediate-range ballistic missile force. He insists that the Pershing IIs and cruise missiles are required to complete the spectrum of deterrence and to couple U.S. long-range strategic forces to the defense of Europe. Others also obviously still hold to the notion that a Euro-strategic balance must exist for deterrence to be complete.

This argument is sometimes stated in terms of a need for NATO to have its own missiles in order to respond to the Soviet SS-20 threat. But the Pershing IIs and ground-launched cruise missiles (GLCMs) would no more be "NATO missiles" than the Trident and Poseidon submarine-launched ballistic missiles (SLBMs) now assigned to NATO defense. They would be exclusively under American control. Indeed, it has been a precondition to their deployment in the Federal Republic of Germany that there would be no West German finger on the button.

As Richard Ullman has observed, however, the argument for the special deterrent efficacy of U.S. INF in Europe is theological rather than logical.[1] And it is hard to argue successfully with another's theology. This is particularly true of ideas about deterrence which, like beauty, lies in the eye of the beholder.

And deterrence itself is a concept that can and does mean different things to different people. To a European, of whichever camp, deterrence of nuclear war is cold comfort if circumstances are created that leave it at all likely that conventional warfare could again engulf the European continent. At a meeting of NATO's Nuclear Planning Group in the late 1960s, the defense ministers of Great

---

[1]Richard Ullman, *The New York Times*, December 29, 1982.

Britain and West Germany were in agreement that special concern about the devastating effects of nuclear weapons should perhaps not be expected from an Englishman who had seen Coventry or a German who had viewed Cologne after their obliteration by nonnuclear means in World War II. But for a citizen of the United States or Canada, the risk of conventional attack produces few nightmares. Deterrence on this side of the Atlantic usually is construed to mean prevention of nuclear war.

In the past, there may have been some virtue in leaving the exact role of nuclear weapons in NATO defense incompletely examined. Many of the participants in the sessions of the NATO Nuclear Planning Group voiced the concern that being too clear about the circumstances in which nuclear weapons might be employed would detract from their broadest deterrent efficacy. There is surely something to be said for an "uncertainty principle" that would leave a potential aggressor unclear as to how far he might go without precipitating a nuclear response. In fact, the current Annual Report to Congress of the Secretary of Defense leaves nothing to conjecture in this regard. It states that the purposes to be served by strategic nuclear forces include that of deterrence "of major conventional attack against U.S. forces and our allies, especially in NATO."[2] This declaratory policy presumably is viewed as gaining greater credibility by prompt deployment of American intermediate-range missiles in Europe, even at a state of development far short of the usual standard for operational systems. The underlying premise is that a nuclear first strike against the Soviet Union is a plausible threat, or that it can be made one by the proposed U.S. INF deployment. I believe the threat to be inherently implausible and thus of no deterrent value.

Those who espouse the contrary view, that nuclear weapons have made for a more peaceful world, often note that there has now been no European war for almost 40 years and that this shows the value of nuclear weapons for extended deterrence—i.e., something beyond mere neutralization of the other side's strategic nuclear arsenal. But in those years there have been wars outside

---

[2] *Report of Secretary of Defense Caspar W. Weinberger to the Congress on FY 1983 Budget, FY 1984 Authorization Request and FY 1983-87 Defense Programs*, February 28, 1982, p. I-18.

Europe where American troops were killed by Soviet-supplied arms—even during the time when the United States had unquestioned nuclear superiority. And it is not hard to list other and better reasons for durable European peace, not least of all the new role of West Germany in the Western Alliance and, of course, the intimate U.S. involvement. It might also be noted that Russian invasion was not the trigger of either of this century's world wars.

Perhaps it would have been wise, or at least not imprudent, to continue to spare NATO's nuclear strategy from too close analysis had not the INF question arisen. But the grave risks of perpetuating the notion that more nuclear weapons in NATO Europe are synonymous with greater security makes it, I believe, advisable now to dissipate the myth of a nuclear nostrum. If kidding ourselves only means kidding our potential adversary as well, the fact that our nuclear doctrine may be unrealistic poses no serious threat to NATO's security. But if adherence to nuclear illusions threatens to promote divisiveness within NATO, to afford the Soviets' protracted opportunity for mischief, and to stimulate Soviet consideration of destabilizing strategies such as launch-on-warning, then it is time to get serious and explicit about the role that nuclear weapons can play in the defense of Western Europe.

Military Inutility of Pershing IIs and Cruise Missiles

For this purpose, I think it is useful first to separate out for special treatment the category of tactical battlefield nuclear weapons. For a couple of decades, these have constituted the vast majority of American nuclear weapons in Europe. Since the removal of the Thors and Jupiters in the early 1960s, only nuclear bombs and missiles on U.S. airplanes have been able to hit Soviet targets from European launching points. But we have maintained thousands of short-range missiles, artillery shells and mines that could be used in the battlefield and adjacent areas. These weapons are obviously unable to strike deep into Eastern Europe or to reach the Soviet Union. Because of their nature, number and placement, their first-use by NATO in the event of a massive conventional attack cannot presently be foreclosed.

But the Pershing II ballistic missiles and ground-launched cruise missiles scheduled to be deployed beginning in December 1983 are in no sense tactical battlefield weapons. They are, in fact, an addition to the strategic forces of the United States. They should not be lumped together with tactical nuclear weapons in an amorphous class of theater nuclear weapons. By the same token, the Soviet SS-20s and the older SS-4s and SS-5s are part of the strategic forces of the Soviet Union and must be considered such by the United States despite their inability to reach targets in the American homeland. Under the North Atlantic Charter an attack on any country in NATO Europe is to be regarded as an attack on the United States itself.

Thus, in considering the possible contribution of American intermediate-range nuclear missiles to NATO defense it is necessary to ask whether the Pershing IIs and GLCMs, along with our ICBMs, SLBMs and strategic bombers, can serve any purpose other than to prevent the Soviet Union from using its nuclear weapons against NATO targets, either in North America or in Europe. Are there indeed any circumstances under which it would serve the national interests of either the United States or its European allies to convert a conventional war into a strategic nuclear exchange? If either the Soviet Union or NATO were to use strategic weapons against the other's homeland, wherever and however these weapons might be launched, the almost inevitable result will be escalation to all-out strategic warfare. In his recently released open letter, Andrei Sakharov gave his view: *"Nuclear weapons only make sense as a means of deterring nuclear aggression by a potential enemy; i.e., a nuclear war cannot be planned with the aim of winning it. Nuclear weapons cannot be viewed as a means of restraining aggression carried out by means of conventional weapons."*[3]

In my opinion, intermediate-range nuclear missiles cannot markedly improve the existing deterrence. If the Soviet Union should strike a European city or a NATO military base with an SS-20, I am confident that the United States would respond in kind, with a Minuteman or Trident missile or an ALCM (air-

---

[3] Andrei Sakharov, "The Danger of Thermonuclear War," *Foreign Affairs*, Summer 1983, p. 1006. Emphasis in original.

launched cruise missile). The initiation of strategic nuclear warfare by the Soviet Union could not go unanswered. The egregiousness of the conduct and the obvious intent to bend the West to Soviet will would make a failure to respond even a greater risk to American security and survival than would a prompt retaliation in kind.

But short of nuclear attack, it is no longer reasonable to base NATO nuclear strategy on the myth that the United States would punish the Soviet Union for non-nuclear aggression by launching a nuclear first strike. This is true today. It will remain just as true when American nuclear warheads can be launched from bases in Western Europe as well as from the Great Plains of the United States and from ballistic missile submarines.

Indeed, the notion that an American president would more readily launch a Pershing II from West Germany than a Minuteman III from our Middle West implies a belief that Soviet retaliation would be against the launching point. It is hard to think of a more "decoupling" assumption. The obvious fact that the Soviet Union would know who owned and operated the offending missile and would react accordingly has been stated flatly and persuasively by Soviet officials, including their military chief, Marshal Nikolai Ogarkov. But the possibility that we might hope to limit the use of nuclear weapons to Eastern and Western Europe quite understandably fuels public alarm in West Germany, Great Britain and elsewhere in Western Europe. Early Reagan Administration suggestions of such a view have not recently been repeated, but the memory is hard to expunge.

The current position of the Reagan Administration appears to be that deterrence is incomplete without European-based missiles "that could reach deep into the Soviet Union, in order to demonstrate that the U.S.S.R. could not devastate Europe from a Russian sanctuary—that attack anywhere in Europe would result in unacceptable damage to the U.S.S.R. itself." The explanation given by Assistant Secretary of State Richard Burt continues:

> The United States took this step in the full knowledge that the Soviet Union would most likely respond to an attack on its homeland by U.S. systems in Europe with an attack on the United States. Thus the emplacement of long-range U.S. cruise and ballistic missiles in Europe makes escalation of any nuclear war in Europe to an intercontinental exchange even more likely.

This is why our allies asked for such a deployment. This is why the United States accepted.[4]

It is not entirely clear whether Burt means that the proposed INF deployment is intended to assure a U.S. nuclear response to a Soviet nuclear attack or whether, in contrast to Dr. Sakharov, he is suggesting that the missiles would be used to respond to conventional aggression as well. In either event, the argument is inconsistent with the credibility of the U.S. defense commitment. Neither the West Europeans nor the Soviets should be given any reason to doubt that Soviet use of nuclear weapons against NATO Europe would trigger U.S. nuclear strikes against Soviet targets. For this purpose, American intermediate-range missiles are unnecessary. For retaliation against Soviet conventional attacks in Europe, they are implausible.

When strategic nuclear weapons, whether of intercontinental or intermediate-range, are seen as serving solely to neutralize the strategic forces of the other side, then the criteria they should meet can, as a military matter, readily be defined. Assured retaliatory capability and strategic stability are best served by strategic forces that are optimized for survivability and present the minimum threat to the survivability of the other side's retaliatory deterrent. They then present the potential aggressor with a force that is neither vulnerable to a preemptive attack nor capable of carrying out a preemptive attack. One of the many ironies of the nuclear age is that it is no longer safe to be able to threaten the substantial attrition of the potential adversary's weapons. The exsistence of such a threat on either side encourages adoption of a launch-on-warning strategy. Your own security is lessened if, at a time of major crisis, the other side must worry that you are about to strike and thus may use its own nuclear weapons rather than take the chance of losing them.

Viewed therefore from a purely military perspective, the proposed ground-launched ballistic missiles and Pershing II ballistic missiles make little, if any, sense. Because of their flight time and unprecedented accuracy, the Pershing IIs can be considered as best

---

[4]Richard Burt, "Nato and Nuclear Deterrence," *Nuclear Weapons in Europe: Modernization and Limitation*, Arms Control Association, Washington, D.C., 1983.

suited for a "decapitating" attack on Soviet command and control centers in Eastern Europe. Although the ground-launched cruise missiles are much slower, their reputed accuracy is comparable. In combination with other planned American systems, such as the MX and the Trident II, or D-5 submarine-launched ballistic missile, they can be seen by the Soviets as contributing to a first strike potential.

The new American intermediate-range forces thus flunk when tested against the criterion of low preemptive strike capability. They do no better in terms of optimum survivability. Indeed, in the event of major confrontation they could be expected to lead the list of targets for Soviet destruction.

The justification for the planned deployment, therefore, is a political one. But it is nonetheless a real one. By substantially expanding the unique nuclear threat to Western Europe, the Soviet Union has presented a challenge that cannot be left unmet. Either the Soviet Union will have to make major cuts in its SS-20s and scuttle the remaining SS-4s and SS-5s that the SS-20s purportedly were designed to replace, or NATO countermeasures specifically designed to respond to this expansion will be undertaken. But because of the fundamental military inutility of U.S. intermediate-range nuclear forces, the nature and scope of the Soviet reductions that may be deemed to make the U.S. deployment politically unnecessary should be left for determination by our Western European allies.

Their decision will obviously be controlled by their evaluation of the role that nuclear weaponry can play in the defense of Europe. But it is not consistent with good faith or with good alliance relations to delude them as to the conditions that would lead to the use of Pershing IIs or ground-launched cruise missiles against the Soviet Union. And in considering the question of when and how American nuclear weapons might be used, it is important to try to make a realistic assessment of the nature of the Soviet threat.

Responding to the Soviet Threat

As has been noted in most of the posture statements of most of the U.S. Secretaries of Defense, a massive Soviet attack on Western Europe is of a high order of unlikelihood. The Soviet Union would know that it would find itself at war with the United States. Whatever time it took and at whatever cost in American lives and money, the Soviets would be driven back. This could be done without nuclear weapons. Moreover, there is every reason to believe that the Soviets understand that they would not be able to maintain political control over the countries of Western Europe. Indeed, there is more going on in Eastern Europe at present than they can handle with any degree of comfort.

There can be little doubt that the Soviet Union would like to be the dominant political force in Western as well as in Eastern Europe. But there can be great doubt that its leaders are so crazed by ideology that they expect or even hope that they could achieve and maintain that dominance by military means. Reasonable minds can differ with Secretary of Defense Caspar Weinberger's view that the threat from the Soviet Union is qualitatively comparable and even graver than that of Hitler's Germany.

What cannot be fully discounted is the chance of limited Soviet aggression to achieve a limited purpose and to do so in a time span that would make NATO response difficult. No one outside the Soviet Union—and probably no one within it—can be confident that internal strains or perceived external opportunities could never trigger a Soviet military move westward. Under some circumstances, a Soviet leader might conclude that he could get away with the limited application of Soviet force in an area important to the West, but one not apt to be considered vital. Under such circumstances, initiation of a strategic nuclear exchange is, for most people at least, an unthinkable response.

Against this least unlikely hypothesis of Soviet aggression, therefore, the important thing is to develop NATO's conventional quick-response capabilities. Here, not only are our strategic nuclear weapons of no value but even the tactical battlefield nuclear weapons are likely either to be unavailable or to be deemed too damaging to NATO population and territory. NATO's conventional power must be such that it is clear to the U.S.S.R. that it cannot expect a short, successful war and must therefore consider whether and how to sustain a protracted war.

As previously noted, U.S. strategic nuclear weapons—those aimed at Soviet targets from air-, sea- and ground-launchers, wherever located—can play no coherent part in NATO defense against conventional attack. It is argued, however, that their very existence produces some inherent inhibitory effect on major military confrontation between East and West. Certainly there can be no guarantee that reason would prevail and great doubt that a major war between East and West could remain limited to conventional arms. Whether or not this is the intended thrust of Assistant Secretary Burt's article, one argument made for the deterrent increment of U.S. intermediate-range nuclear forces is that their presence in Europe would make conventional war impossible. It can as readily be argued, however, that this added escalatory potential would deter NATO from defending itself, at least against a limited Soviet conventional attack. In any event, the risks that nuclear weapons create greatly outweigh any incremental benefit that can be claimed for them in deterring conventional war.

It is moreover highly conjectural that whatever oblique and nebulous form of "extended deterrence" nuclear weapons may be deemed to provide, anything can be gained from the development and deployment of categories beyond the existing strategic systems. The fact that a major conventional conflict can readily escalate to a nuclear exchange inescapably must induce caution on the part of the nuclear superpowers. But since the risk is mutual, as would be the devastation of each side's societies, strategic nuclear weapons provide nothing exploitable in theory or in practice. It is not necessary, not I believe even possible, to accept the thesis that nuclear war can be fought "rationally" to achieve foreign policy objectives.[5]

In fact, if not in generally accepted theory, both nuclear superpowers are compelled to a "no-first-strike" policy. The current leaders of the United States and the Soviet Union have asserted, as did their predecessors, their recognition that there can be no winners in a nuclear war. No matter what the scale of a Soviet conventional attack, a NATO response that involved the explosion of warheads on Soviet territory could only turn possible short-term territorial loss into total devastation, at least of Western Europe, and probably of the United States as well.

---

[5]For the classic exposition of this thesis, see Colin Gray and Keith Payne, "Victory is Possible," *Foreign Policy*, Summer 1980.

A recently reported top secret State Department document is said to warn that existing submarine-launched ballistic missiles assigned to NATO cannot do the INF job because "they are generally regarded as strategic systems whose use prior to General Nuclear Response might convey an overly escalatory signal to the Soviet Union."[6] The notion that the Soviet leaders would take a first strike with Pershing IIs or GLCMs less seriously would be laughable if it were not so dangerous.

The conclusion that no-first-strike is, though unannounced, a fact of life in the nuclear age does not necessarily mean that both sides also have a tacit policy of "no-first-use." The Soviet Union has offered such a guarantee. The United States has declined to go along.

Battlefield Nuclear Weapons

The considerations involved in the possible use of battlefield nuclear weapons are analytically different from those involved in strategic arms. Unlike intercontinental- and intermediate-range missiles, the thousands of tactical nuclear weapons deployed in NATO Europe do not threaten the Soviet homeland. As to these weapons, the Soviets have a perfect defense: unless they invade, tactical nuclear arms can never destroy Russian lives or Russian property.

Declaratory NATO strategy has long been based on the use of tactical nuclear weapons to deter or deflect a massive Soviet armored assault. Unlike the ephemeral and undefinable inhibition that strategic weapons may place on major conventional warfare, the scenario for use of the battlefield nuclear missiles and shells is both concrete and plausible. They could be used with stunning effect against massed Soviet tanks and troops. Moreover, unlike a strategic attack, such use would not inescapably invite a nuclear response. This show of NATO's determination to resist, even if it means exploding nuclear devices on NATO territory, could quite conceivably compel Soviet reconsideration and withdrawal.

---

[6] Jack Anderson, "Report Bares NATO Forces' Deficiencies," *The Washington Post*, September 8, 1983.

The costs and risks of first-use of battlefield nuclear weapons, however, should not be discounted. The decision to employ them would be extraordinarily difficult. Unless simply a token use were sufficient to discourage Soviet pursuit of the attack, the numbers necessary to inflict significant damage on the attacker would wreak incalculable havoc on the defenders' own territory. Many of our most experienced military leaders, such as General Maxwell Taylor and Admiral Noel Gayler, have expressed their inability to devise plans for using such weapons. Vice Admiral Gerald E. Miller, who served as Deputy Director of the Joint Strategic Target Planning Staff, has said: "The simple fact is that nuclear weapons are not very realistic tools for any military commander."[7] These views are in striking contrast to those expressed in a recent article by retired French Colonel Marc Geneste, Vice President of the Center for Study of Total Strategy in Paris. Colonel Geneste contends: "It is clear that in terms of tactical effects, deterrence, damage and cost effectiveness, neutron shells are preferable to conventional forces. It is the cheap answer to the superiority of Soviet land forces."[8]

This answer may not be so cheap. The line between strategic and tactical nuclear weapons can become blurred and even disappear if NATO's defensive use is matched by the Soviets. Once Russian nuclear warheads start exploding in Western Europe it will be hard to preserve the distinction between tactical and strategic. The use of Soviet nuclear weapons against NATO forces in NATO territory would call for the use of American nuclear weapons against military targets in the Soviet Union itself. The escalatory dangers therefore dictate that no heavy reliance be placed on NATO's battlefield nuclear weapons for the defense of West European territory.

In this regard, the controversy over the so-called neutron bomb—the enhanced radiation nuclear weapon—illustrates the fact that the questions raised by the presence of American nuclear weapons in Europe are at least as much political as they are military. Supporters of the neutron bomb, like Colonel Geneste, see it

---

[7] *The Washington Spectator*, August 15, 1983.
[8] Marc Geneste, "Why the Allies Need the Neutron Bomb," *The Wall Street Journal*, August 17, 1983.

as an important addition to NATO's security because of its ability to kill enemy personnel with minimal damage to West European infrastructure. Opponents feel that it will lower the nuclear threshold, because it is more apt to be used than the current, more widely destructive, nuclear weaponry. As a practical matter, however, the decision to use a neutron weapon would probably be no easier than if only the older type of tactical nuclear weapons were available. The fact that it might kill more Russians and fewer West Germans is not apt to make Soviet nuclear retaliation less likely. From the military standpoint it would seem wiser to concentrate on high technology, non-nuclear systems that hold great promise of making the tank obsolete.

The handling of the neutron bomb issue, however, is a case history on how not to run an alliance. The on-again, off-again treatment of the weapon gave a good deal of impetus to the INF decision at the end of 1979. The U.S. Government was determined to show its willingness to send additional nuclear arms to Western Europe. But the neutron bomb debacle should lead U.S. officals to accept the fact that the ultimate decision on INF deployment, and on what Soviet concessions might be accepted as making the deployment unnecessary, is one for our European allies.

An Arms Control Solution for INFs

As previously stated, I can see no military need for 572 additional warheads to strike Soviet targets. Indeed, I believe that their installation in West Germany, in particular, will mean less, rather than greater, European security. But if our European friends continue to want them, and if no arms control alternative can be developed that they find preferable, then the deployment, in my opinion, should proceed.

We have to expect that deployment will mean demonstrations and perhaps violence in the Federal Republic of Germany and possibly in Italy and the United Kingdom as well. Dutch and Belgian governments are apt never to put their publics to the test by authorizing acceptance of the American missiles. In any event the issue will be a long-lasting and divisive one for the Alliance. It may mean the growth of increased anti-American and anti-NATO sentiment. But at this stage a unilateral American decision to forego the deployment would mean a neutron bomb type controversy that would reinforce doubts about American leadership and American resolve. Moreover, an uncompensated cancellation of the proposed INF deployment would in effect give the Soviets a veto power over a NATO weapons decision.

The facts that the deployment will be drawn out and that the Pershing IIs and ground-launched cruise missiles may still be many months away from true operational capability offer an opportunity still for an arms control solution. We owe it to ourselves and to our allies to make a genuine effort to bring one about. As previously noted, the late 1979 dual-track decision committed us to do so.

It is, I believe, completely unrealistic to expect that the Soviets would accept either the zero-zero option initially proposed or the later offer of President Reagan to deploy only the number of U.S. warheads that the Soviet Union elects to retain in its force of SS-20s, SS-4s and SS-5s. Although we cannot, of course, negotiate restrictions on British and French nuclear weapons, we also cannot expect that the Soviets will ignore their existence. Vice President George Bush recently acknowledged to reporters that West European missile forces must be addressed and answers found "somewhere along the line."[9]

If we put ourselves in the Soviets' position—a tough job, but one that's unavoidable in assessing negotiability—we must conclude that we would not be impressed by arguments that the British and French forces are "strategic" in purported contrast to our GLCMs and Pershing IIs, or that the Soviets cannot claim any right to have as many intermediate-range weapons as all the other countries. From their standpoint, the U.S., British and French forces pose a combined threat. They see us as being, in truth, an alliance and cannot be expected to place any credence in suggestions that the British and French missiles are "independent" and cannot be taken into account.

I also wonder whether those who make this argument have considered its implications. If British and French national security re-

---

[9] Don Oberdorfer, "Bush Says Talks Cannot Ignore British Missiles," *The Washington Post,* September 29, 1983.

quire separate nuclear forces, uncommitted to NATO defense, what does this suggest for the Federal Republic of Germany? The logic of the argument, to the extent any exists, can only increase European concerns about "decoupling" and encourage proliferation.

Nor can we expect that the Soviets will permit us to negotiate arms control restrictions that will benefit the People's Republic of China. Yet in calling either for complete abolition of Soviet INFs or for reduction to a global level that the United States can match by itself, we demand that the Soviets ignore not only the British and French missiles but also those of the Chinese.

In his speech to the U.N. General Assembly on September 26, 1983, President Reagan announced certain further revisions in the American position. He picked up on Soviet suggestions that a ceiling on warheads might be negotiable and said that the United States would not insist on matching, in its European deployments, the entire global Soviet intermediate-range missile force. Instead, he indicated that the United States would be prepared to match in Europe only those Soviet warheads targeted against Europe, but would reserve the right to deploy elsewhere intermediate-range missiles equal to those targeted by the Soviet Union against Asia. In addition, he proclaimed a willingness to include limits on bombers in an INF agreement and, if the Soviets reduced their intermediate-range nuclear force, to cut back the planned Pershing II deployment to maintain proportionately the same mix of Pershing IIs and ground-launched cruise missiles.

As thus revised, however, the American position still fails to address the Soviets' major objections. It still insists that the Soviets approve some deployment of U.S. missiles in West Germany and other NATO countries unless the U.S.S.R. eliminates a category of nuclear weaponry it has maintained for over 20 years. The chances are slim that the Soviets will accept a plan that denies them the ability to maintain even a balance with the non-American nuclear forces that face them, particularly when these forces are about to be strengthened. The French and British have announced intentions to increase their missile warheads about fourfold. The Chinese are testing a new submarine-launched ballistic missile and already have land-based ballistic missiles of sufficent range to strike any Soviet target.

It may be instructive to consider what our stance would be if the Chinese nuclear weapons were aimed at the United States instead of at Russia. Few Americans would accept the contention that we would not then have a right to match the combined Russian and Chinese nuclear forces. Lest this seem too wildly hypothetical, it might be recalled that in late 1967 the threat of a Chinese missile attack was the principal justification for the original Anti-Ballistic Missile program.

It was too much to hope that the Soviet Union would find this peripheral adjustment in the American position to be an acceptable basis for resolution of the INF impasses. Soviet leader Andropov promptly made it clear that it was not and accused the United States, in a signed statement released by TASS on September 28, of being embarked on a "militarist course that poses a grave threat to peace."[10]

At the core of the problem is the fact that there is little prospect of a comprehensive resolution of the INF issue when these talks ignore the overall strategic context in which intermediate-range missiles must be considered. For example, President Reagan announced about two years ago a strategic program that would include the MX, the Trident II or D-5 submarine-launched ballistic missile with hard silo destroying capability and the sea-launched cruise missile. The Soviets are thus being asked to scrap all or most of their SS-20s in return for a U.S. undertaking not to deploy 108 Pershing IIs and 464 ground-launched cruise missiles while the United States retains the option to deploy some 4,000 sea-launched cruise missiles.

The elimination of Soviet intermediate-range nuclear weapons can only be negotiated in a bargaining forum in which all of the strategic weapons systems are available for discussion and for trade-offs. The separate status of the INF talks is the result of expedience rather than logic. The European revulsion against the nuclear arms race predated the peaking of the American nuclear freeze movement. In an effort to lessen opposition to the proposed INF deployment, the Reagan Administration began the INF talks in November of 1981. Thus, about two years after the NATO

---

[10] Reprinted in *The New York Times*, September 29, 1983, p. A14.

dual-track decision on intermediate-range nuclear forces and about two years before the proposed deployment, the second part of that decision was finally operational. But it must still be questioned whether the arms control alternative has been effectively and resolutely pursued.

There have been indications that some compromise, at least of an interim nature, might be feasible. The much advertised "walk in the woods" discussions between Ambassador Paul Nitze and his Soviet counterpart Yuli Kvitsinsky in July of 1982 may have been an aberration or a misunderstanding. But it is difficult for those familiar with the limits placed on Soviet negotiators to assume that Kvitsinsky was acting solely on his own. At the same time, the proposition seems so favorable to the West as almost to be too good to be true. American and Soviet intermediate-range nuclear forces would, under its rumored terms, have been in virtual balance.

For many years up to 1977, the Soviets had between 600 and 700 warheads on their intermediate-range missiles. Anything that would approximately restore the status quo, by scrapping the remaining SS-4s and SS-5s and by destroying significant numbers of SS-20s, should be acceptable to our West European allies and hence to us. This would involve no political retreat from the NATO dual-track decision of December 1979. At that time, the Soviets had about 400 SS-4s and SS-5s and some 200 SS-20s. A return to a 600 Soviet INF warhead total would mean an acutal reduction in the nuclear threat to Western Europe as compared with the past two decades. The remaining 200 Soviet SS-20s would in all likelihood be split about equally between those aimed at Asian targets and those directed toward NATO Europe. Both in numbers of warheads and in megatonnage, therefore, a significant reduction would have been achieved.

Soviet President Yuri Andropov has repeatedly affirmed Soviet willingness to remove and destroy some of the SS-20s now directed against NATO Europe if the Pershing II and GLCM deployment is cancelled. American officials have been quoted as saying that there can be no deal that doesn't recognize the American right to equality with the Soviet Union in intermediate-range missiles. This position finds continued support from some European quarters. In late August, the influential West German newspaper, *Die*

Welt, found in Andropov's proposal a design "to keep America's efficient weapons technology out of Europe." The article then asked: "What, after all, will America's role be in Western Europe if it is forbidden to modernize and thus be condemned to military inferiority?"[11] The answer is that the proposed American missiles have nothing to do with usable military capability.

Of course no interim agreement was reached and the U.S. missile deployment began on schedule. Reagan Administration officials still maintain that, faced with the fact that protests and demonstrations have failed to block the missiles, the Soviet Union will commence serious negotiations. According to Secretary of Defense Weinberger, the deployment "will be the only thing to make the Soviets realize that they indeed should negotiate."[12] But the history of the American-Soviet nuclear arms competition shows that introduction of new weapons leads to countermeasures rather than compromise or capitulation.

In the late 1950s, even the groundless boasts of Nikita Khrushchev created fears of a "missile gap" that spurred the accumulation of U.S. ICBMs and the invention of the Polaris submarine. Deployment of MIRVed missiles (i.e, missiles equipped with multiple independently-targetable reentry vehicles) in 1969 was expected by some U.S. officals to give us bargaining leverage in the SALT I negotiations. What it gave us instead in a few years was the MIRVing of Soviet ICBMs and the theoretical "window of vulnerability."

Soviet officals now say that they will respond to the U.S. cruise and Pershing II missiles with deployments that will pose a comparable threat to Western Europe and the United States itself. No doubt they will take some such action. I think we need not worry about efforts to place Soviet missiles in countries in the Western Hemisphere. The Politburo is not likely to authorize a replay of the 1962 Cuban missile crisis in the knowledge that propinquity and American naval capability would bring about another major Soviet embarrassment. And neither Fidel Castro nor the Sandi-

---

[11] *Die Welt,* August 29, 1983, as reported in the *German Press Review,* Embassy of the Federal Republic of Germany, August 31, 1983.
[12] *The Washington Times,* October 4, 1983, p. 7A.

nista government is apt to make a move that would invite and justify direct American military action in Cuba or Nicaragua.

But SS-20s might be stationed in remote parts of the Soviet Union that would enable them to reach American targets in the far Northwest. And increased Soviet submarine patrols close to our coasts, with missiles perhaps tested in a depressed trajectory, would enable Soviet weapons to reach strategic targets in the United States in times comparable to those of the Pershing IIs. Cruise missiles on Soviet surface ships are another discouraging possibility. The stationing of more and improved Soviet nuclear missiles in East Germany and other Warsaw Pact countries is now a virtual certainty.

The Soviet Union staged a dramatic walkout in Geneva in November 1983, as it warned it would. The beginning of the installation of the U.S. missiles in West Germany, Sicily and the United Kingdom seems to have effectively ended the separate existence of the INF talks. The prospect that deployment might somehow be avoided is what kept this unnaturally restricted bargaining forum alive. But the termination of these talks need not be fatal to the prospects for eventual reduction of Soviet SS-20s. The issue of European intermediate-range nuclear forces could and should then be folded into the negotiations on the longer range strategic forces. In that forum, the French and British missiles will reassume their relatively minor stature. As compared with the many thousands of strategic warheads in the U.S. and Soviet arsenals, they will not loom large enough to frustrate agreement on substantial reductions and qualitative controls.

The end of INF negotiations can thus provide an opportunity to get nuclear arms control back on the track. It was contemplated throughout the SALT II negotiations that intermediate-range nuclear forces would be included as part of the next round of strategic arms talks. As noted above, the Protocol to the SALT II treaty permitted testing of ground- and sea-launched missiles but prohibited their deployment through 1981. Their fate thereafter was to depend upon success in limiting Soviet intermediate-range missiles. The Joint Statement of Principles and Basic Guidelines for Subsequent Negotiations on the Limitation of Strategic Arms specified that the major objectives would be significant and substantial reductions, qualitative limitations, including restrictions on new types and on modernization of existing types of nuclear weapons, and resolution of the Protocol issues.

These should continue to be our negotiating objectives. They can be achieved by building on the foundation that has already been established and, in particular, by negotiating substantial reductions in the ceilings and subceilings established by the SALT II treaty. The INF problem can be resolved by including this category of strategic weaponry under a common ceiling and thus subject to similar phased reductions.

This is the approach taken in a recent proposal that I co-authored with Ambassador Gerard Smith, the U.S. negotiator of the SALT I agreements, and John Rhinelander, Legal Advisor during the SALT I negotiations.[13] Specifically, it calls for a first phase in which reductions would be made in the aggregate limits on strategic nuclear delivery vehicles (from 2,400 to 1,800) and in the ceiling on launchers of MIRVed ICBMs and SLBMs (from 1,200 to 880). In addition, the ceiling on MIRVed launchers of ICBMs would be cut in half (from 820 to 410) and that on the Soviet heavy missiles—the SS-18s—would be reduced from 308 to 150. This would go a long way toward achieving major goals professed by the Reagan Administration—to lower Soviet throw-weight and MIRVed ICBM numbers.

This proposal indulged the hope that an interim agreement might be achieved in the first phase that would require essentially the restoration of the INF warhead balance as it existed prior to development of SS-20s. This would mean a total global force of no more than 200 SS-20s. Thereafter, in a second phase, INF and START would be combined and common ceilings established from which further reductions would take place. There would be added an overall limit on the total number of nuclear weapons (missile warheads and bombs) applicable to both intercontinental and intermediate-range forces. With a collapse of the INF talks, the proposed first phase would, of course, be bypassed.

The inclusion of intermediate-range nuclear forces under launcher and warhead ceilings, subject to phased reductions,

---

[13] Released at a press luncheon of the Arms Control Association, Washington, D.C., September 27, 1983.

would have the side benefit of creating strong pressures against the maintenance of Soviet missiles that present a unique threat to NATO Europe. SS-20s would be lumped with MIRVed ICBMs. This might require some increases in the proposed new lower ceilings. But Soviet planners would be reluctant to use up a significant part of a dwindling entitlement on missiles that could not reach U.S. targets. Similarly, U.S. planners would have to consider whether any part of the U.S. entitlement should be wasted on weapons that are less survivable and less stabilizing than those of intercontinental range.

If Soviet shorter range missiles have been moved to Eastern Europe, the agreement should provide for their immediate removal and a freeze on these and comparable U.S. weapons.

What we and our NATO allies must decide is whether we will be better off with more nuclear weapons of our own or with fewer Soviet nuclear weapons. It should be clear that we can't have both. But an intelligent decision cannot be made so long as the decision-makers cling to the idea that "modernization" of the U.S. nuclear arsenal in Western Europe contains some special deterrent magic.

Although a short-term setback seems likely, the longer range prospects for nuclear arms control are good if we are prepared to heed Andrei Sakharov's advice that for arms control talks to be successful "the West should have something that it can give up." If a Pershing II, or an MX, or a Trident II is considered too good to lose, then its value as a bargaining chip will be lost, along with chances of reducing the Soviet nuclear threat.

Karsten D. Voigt

Nuclear Weapons in Europe: A German Social Democrat's Perspective

Widespread demonstrations against the mounting level of armaments in the East and West are no cause for alarm. What is truly alarming is that since the end of World War II, politicians have succeeded in neither eliminating war and the danger of war nor worldwide arms buildups.

In Europe, memories of the horrors of the First and Second World Wars are deeply rooted in the consciousness of nations. Anyone living, as do the Germans, along the borders separating the NATO countries from the Warsaw Pact nations is aware that even a war waged solely with conventional weapons leaves few chances of survival. This is all the more true of a war fought with nuclear weapons—even if "only" with so-called tactical nuclear weapons, of which many thousands are stored in Europe. Their combat use would convert large parts of Europe into desert. In these regions the survivors would indeed envy the dead.

War is thus no longer a suitable vehicle by which to conduct the East-West struggle. Efforts at the peaceful accommodation of interests, the control and reduction of armaments, and military confidence-building measures must receive political priority. To be sure, such efforts presuppose the development of an adequate deterrent; but this must be sharply distinguished from the capabilities required to wage war and win it. The long-term objective must be focused on turning potential military opponents into partners seeking a common security.

During the 1970s, East-West détente resulted in an appreciable decrease in the fear of war. In particular, better relations between the United States and the Soviet Union, the Four-Power Agreement on Berlin, the Federal Republic of Germany's treaties with its Eastern neighbors, the first Strategic Arms Limitation Treaty (SALT I), as well as the confidence-building measures stipulated in the Conference on Security and Cooperation in Europe's (CSCE) Final Document—all contributed to making Western Europe one of the most politically stable security areas in the world. Building upon what had been achieved, it was hoped that a SALT II accord would be reached and that progress would be made at the MBFR (Mutual and Balanced Force Reduction) negotiations in Vienna. Détente was to be broadened and intensified, not questioned.

Overall, for Europeans the evolution of détente and its present prospects provide no cause for disappointment. Notwithstanding the Warsaw Pact's enormous military potential, there are no signs the Soviet Union currently poses an acute military threat to Western Europe. It shows no desire to expand militarily into Western Europe. Given NATO's capabilities, such an attempt would pose incalculable risks for the Soviet Union.

There is, consequently, no basis for the mounting concern that the decision on intermediate-range nuclear force (INF) modernization will determine conclusively whether the Soviet Union will achieve hegemony over Western Europe. The Soviet Union cannot credibly and successfully use its military potential to blackmail Western Europe politically. Besides, the experience of the entire postwar period shows—and this holds true especially for West Berlin and the Federal Republic—that such attempts have been unsuccessful. Any effort to use the SS-20 missiles to blackmail or bully Western Europe would elicit a strong counter-response. However, members of the peace movement who oppose the INF deployments because they believe the new missiles will provoke the Soviets into taking dangerous countermeasures, unwittingly lend credence to arguments that the U.S.S.R. is successfully blackmailing Western Europe.

During the 1970s, it was in the United States that disappointment with détente developed and deepened as the Soviet Union accelerated its arms buildup while American defense expenditures declined after the Vietnam war ended. Washington's perception of a growing strategic imbalance produced a more pessimistic assessment of the Soviet Union's intentions and military capabilities than that held by Europeans. This pessimism deepened in the wake of differences over SALT II, the crisis in Iran, and the Soviet intervention in Afghanistan.

For 35 years, there has been no expansion of the Soviet sphere of influence in Europe. West Europeans have no fear that domestic communist parties loyal to Moscow will come to power; rather it is the East European regimes that must contend with the credibility crises affecting Marxist-Leninist ideology. The problem confronting Europe today is less that of containing Soviet military expansion (unlike, for example, Afghanistan), than of organizing lasting, peaceful East-West coexistence in the face of continuing conflict between the two political systems.

This was the situation perceived in Europe when former West German Chancellor Helmut Schmidt delivered his now famous 1977 address to the International Institute for Strategic Studies (IISS). Although that speech was much quoted with respect to the eventual NATO dual-track decision, most of it was devoted to the economic problems of industrial nations and the world as a whole, not to the problem of SS-20s. Two years later Schmidt compared the then-current world situation to the time of the outbreak of the First World War. Interestingly, he viewed the risk of a Soviet attack against NATO in the late 1970s and early 1980s as small, while he saw a growing risk of war in the uncontrolled escalation of crises, in faulty crisis management, and in misperceptions and erroneous decisions. His reference to 1914 was designed to stimulate comparisons with the current international situation on another point: how an unforeseeable incident on the fringes of the then-centers of political and military power—the assassination at Sarajevo—triggered the outbreak of that war.

Since the late 1970s Europeans have worried less that a war between East and West might erupt in Europe than that conflicts on their perimeter or beyond might spill over onto their continent and finally involve them against their will in an East-West nuclear confrontation. These NATO countries, already exposed to extraordinary political and military dangers given their geographical location, did not wish in addition to be linked against their will to military risks outside Europe. Their fears have been further fueled by discussions on the possibility of a regional extension of NATO's sphere of responsibility. They have thereby revived an old demand for the right of veto over the use of nuclear weapons by the states on whose territory American nuclear weapons are located. Of course, fears that U.S. military activities around the globe might spill over into Western Europe are difficult to square with often-repeated West European anxieties that the United States will decouple itself from European security. Nevertheless it would be a grave mistake, one which would put the cohesion of NATO into question, if the United States were to make its military guarantee for Western Europe dependent on NATO's support for U.S. military engagements outside the NATO area in Asia, Africa or Latin America.

Flexible Response: How Valid?

Considering the military-strategic and political situation in the 1960s and 1970s, flexible response formed an appropriate approach to maintaining the credibility of the American commitment to Europe. Given current military-strategic conditions, a decrease in the number of nuclear weapons and their military functions as prescribed in the doctrine of flexible response is desirable for the 1980s.

When the European NATO partners agreed to the doctrine of flexible response, they viewed it in the context of their particular interests. Specifically, given its nuclear component, it was seen as cheaper and as requiring less territory than the training and deployment of conventional forces would have necessitated. Also, from a European perspective, it was important to confront the Warsaw Pact powers, were they to attack, with the risk of nuclear war. A potential aggressor had to realize that even what was initially a conventional attack could very quickly lead to nuclear counterstrikes. The risk of rapid nuclear escalation from tactical to strategic nuclear weapons was never completely excluded.

For the United States there was an obvious interest in having options that were credible, that is, realizable, without having to trigger an automatic escalation all the way up to strategic nuclear warfare and thus involving the risk of its own destruction. In contrast to the strategy of massive retaliation, the controlled use of nuclear weapons within the framework of flexible response increased the credibility of the U.S. deterrent posture. Moreover, the possibility of nuclear escalation linked the United States and Western Europe in a common risk and thereby strengthened the security and political unity of NATO.

The contradictions and conflicting interests inherent in the strategy of flexible response have never been fully discussed. They have been covered over by a NATO doctrine that views the resulting strategic ambiguity as an added factor of risk and thus an additional element of deterrence against the Warsaw Pact. But this is of dubious value for Alliance politics: it presents the Soviet Union with the opportunity to exploit unresolved conflicts of interest among the Atlantic allies thereby causing considerable strain in the Alliance.

Currently, public discussion in Europe, as in the United States, focuses above all on the risk of nuclear warfare and its consequences. Europeans and Americans are equally afraid of a worldwide nuclear holocaust. But their fears give rise to different specific concerns. Many Europeans are afraid that the two nuclear superpowers might think it possible to launch and wage a controlled *regional* nuclear war. By contrast, many Americans are worried that their government, by insisting upon the threat of a first-use of nuclear weapons in case of a conventional attack limited to Western Europe, might erroneously believe that it can control and limit a war to Europe once it has started. Underestimating the risk of a general escalation of a nuclear war beginning in Europe would, as some Americans see it, carelessly endanger the fate of all mankind and of their own countrymen in particular.

These differing views and interests are, obviously, a reflection of differences in geographic location. NATO's doctrine of flexible response was designed to reconcile them. But, in fact, the possibility of limiting and quickly ending any East-West conflict, once it has broken out in Central Europe, is questionable. In their analysis of possible conflict scenarios, many Western experts consider a limitation, regionalization and, finally, termination of a nuclear war impossible even in theory. The doctrine of flexible response, in their view, is nothing but a sort of esoteric game devoid of any connection with the reality of the actual course of a military conflict between East and West.

This analysis carries all the more weight since the declared Soviet military strategy assumes that, once started, a conflict would be fought with all available weapons, including nuclear ones. In any event, official Soviet statements do not envisage selective or limited nuclear wars. On the contrary, the possibility of limiting nuclear wars is decisively rejected. On this point, Soviet leaders agree with Clausewitz, who stressed time and again that there are no limits in war. Yet notwithstanding this declared military doctrine, the Soviet Union has developed both intermediate- and short-range battlefield nuclear weapons that give it the option of waging a limited nuclear war.

The validity of the concept of flexible response must thus remain questionable. Even if the United States and the Soviet Union were technically capable of destroying part of their opponent's nuclear arsenal with a limited strike, they could still not foresee the consequences of such an action; in particular, they could not rule out from the beginning that the conflict would not escalate into a global nuclear war.

A controlled response following a limited attack with strategic nuclear weapons is improbable if only for political-institutional and political-psychological reasons. The belief of some military planners that the escalation of a war, once under way, could be restrained and that in the thick of the struggle they would be free and able to terminate the fighting and de-escalate in a controlled fashion, is just an article of faith—nothing else. So long as it is even faintly conceivable that a threat of selective nuclear strikes could lead to a major nuclear war and thus to mutual destruction, the threat itself—by rational standards—is not credible.

Within the framework of flexible response, European strategy must combine a dual role. In the case of a Soviet attack on Western Europe, the NATO allies should have the capacity (not compulsion) to respond selectively. At the same time, they must safeguard the NATO triad—i.e., conventional weapons, theater nuclear weapons and strategic nuclear weapons—to maintain credible deterrence. And in order to emphasize this integration with global strategic deterrence, the Euro-strategic nuclear forces must remain under the control of the United States.

The most important military-strategic reason for NATO's dual-track decision of December 12, 1979 (to deploy Pershing II and cruise missiles while simultaneously pursuing arms control negotiations) was to reestablish the capacity for controlled nuclear escalation. The deployment of these weapons will give NATO the means to carry out selective missions against military targets well inside the Warsaw Pact territory. But the small number of missiles involved, the limitation of their range, and the evident intention to minimize corollary damage indicate to the potential opponent that military restraint will be observed in the event of conflict. This requires a high degree of reliability, penetration capacity, and accuracy on the part of the intermediate-range weapons.

Yet advocates of NATO modernization frequently overestimate the added credibility that will result from putting the December 1979 decision into effect. They overestimate the addition to deterrence of the new weapons and the corresponding additional protection from political blackmail. But even blackmail via intermediate-range weapons can succeed only if it is credible. Military threats with intermediate-range nuclear forces, however, are not credible, because their realization continues to involve an unacceptable risk of global war for the blackmailer.

Given the possibility of regionally limited nuclear wars, it should be recognized that there are greater risks arising from nuclear artillery, short-range, and other battlefield nuclear weapons than from intermediate-range nuclear weapons. The risk inherent in the deployment of new weapons stems from the fact that they appear to encourage war-fighting and thereby weaken deterrence. The defensive intent associated with the new weapons technology must be made politically clear, for the development of this technology has so far not been blocked by treaty agreement. To this end, a policy of détente and, more specifically, arms control agreements are a necessary means.

Governments that are not actively pursuing a policy of détente and seeking arms control will repeatedly have to allay doubts as to whether their goal of preventing war corresponds to the objective results of their policies. For this, if for no other reason, the West should give priority to a satisfactory agreement aimed at reducing European nuclear arsenals over the deployment of new intermediate-range weapons.

Pershing IIs and Cruise Missiles: Arms Control Outcomes

Arms control agreements have hitherto rarely produced reductions of weapons systems already in place. Moreover, arms control policy has been in crisis since the U.S. failure to ratify SALT II. East-West relations have deteriorated. Hence the peace movement seeks new and promising avenues that will lead to arms reductions. The peace movement sees one such avenue in significant, unilateral—but time-limited—prior concessions. Such concessions on the part of the West would be coupled with an invitation to the East to follow suit. Building on this beginning, further negotiations on verifiable agreements could proceed.

Under certain circumstances prior unilateral concessions, provided they do not jeopardize security, can foster negotiations. Unfortunately, these conditions were not present at the Geneva INF negotiations. The U.S.S.R. contended that a balance existed between NATO and the Warsaw Pact with respect to intermediate-range weapons. But prior to the U.S. deployments in November 1983, these weapons had not been placed in Western Europe; NATO therefore speaks of a Soviet monopoly. Both contentions reflect one-sided definitions of security and balance. What is considered "catching up" to NATO appears as "forging ahead" to Moscow. Given this point of departure, a unilateral renunciation by NATO of its planned deployment of Pershing IIs and cruise missiles, not linked to any Soviet reductions, would be viewed by Moscow, not as a prior concession, but as a confirmation of its past positions.

When Soviet President Yuri Andropov agreed to scrap a considerable number of SS-20s if the United States would abandon deployment of intermediate-range weapons, the U.S.S.R. modified its earlier assertion that a balance in this weapons category already existed. This was an important positive step. According to information given to the author by Soviet officials in September 1983, Andropov's proposal meant that the Soviet Union was willing to cut back 311 of its 473 missiles in Europe, including about 90 of its 250 SS-20s which can target Western Europe from areas east of the Urals. The remaining 162 SS-20s are seen as compensation for British and French missiles.

More recently the Soviet Union has declared it will deploy new missiles in Eastern Europe should Pershing IIs and cruise missiles be deployed in Western Europe. Thereby the Soviet Union underscores its contention that the United States would have the advantage if it carried out its planned deployments.

Such a Soviet move might be an attempt to legitimize the modernization of FROG (free rocket over ground), Scaleboard and Scud missiles through the deployment of a new generation of missiles (SS-21s, SS-22s and SS-23s). This interpretation is corroborated by the fact that Soviet officials have informed the author that the U.S.S.R. is willing to commit itself not to introduce these missiles should the West relinquish Pershing IIs and cruise missiles. Whether the Soviet Union is really prepared to do this can only be determined through negotiations. The Soviet Union has not offered to renounce the deployment of short-range nuclear systems if NATO renounces its planned deployment of new intermediate-range missiles. Without subscribing to the Soviet interpretation of who has the advantage, the West should press the Soviet Union to clarify under what conditions it would waive the introduction of the SS-21s, SS-22s and SS-23s and similar types of weapons in the future.

Even if the United States were to renounce unilaterally the deployment of land-based, intermediate-range weapons in Western Europe, the West would still possess a sufficient nuclear deterrent. But for primarily *political* reasons NATO should not agree to renounce such deployments until the Soviet Union is ready to reduce its nuclear armaments adequately.

The nature and extent of such Soviet reductions must be established through negotiations: if Moscow will only agree to small reductions in SS-20 deployments, it should compensate by greater reductions of shorter range nuclear systems or by relevant concessions in the area of strategic weapons. Should Moscow recognize that it has more than enough SS-20s deployed (which is highly unlikely) and announce that it will make unilateral reductions, the West could then demonstrate its readiness for a partial or total renunciation of deployment, depending on the extent of the unilateral Soviet reductions.

Prospects for an accord rendering unnecessary the deployment of new land-based, intermediate-range weapons in return for a dramatic reduction of SS-20s are minimal for obvious political reasons. The deployments have begun and the Soviets have withdrawn from the INF talks. At the Geneva negotiations, the points at issue were defined clearly and unambiguously. But essentially they still remain points at issue. The Soviet Union insists on including the British and French strategic systems in its count. The United States objects. If this controversy remains unresolved, no agreement leading to the complete abandonment of Pershing II and cruise missile deployments can be expected in the foreseeable future.

Both in Moscow and in Washington, the results of the "walk in the woods" discussions between Paul Nitze and Yuli Kvitsinsky, head of the American and Soviet delegations respectively, met with disapproval and rejection. This is unfortunate, because during their walk Nitze and Kvitsinsky discussed the option of a substantial reduction in the deployment of SS-20s in return for U.S. agreement to forego Pershing IIs and reduce the deployment of cruise missiles. This would have been an acceptable compromise.

A fully satisfactory accord should include a Soviet commitment to drastically reduce its SS-20s and a U.S. renunciation of Pershing II and cruise missile deployments. Such an accord would have been negotiable as long as there was no U.S. deployment of new weapons. Now that deployments have begun, is there any hope for such a negotiated accord? To suppose the Soviet Union would be prepared to make considerably greater concessions after Western deployments than before is highly unrealistic. If Soviet conviction of the certainty of deployments were the necessary precondition for a satisfactory, negotiated accord, the chances for such an agreement would now be ideal. Evidently they are not.

It would, moreover, run contrary to all political experience that the West, after having commenced Pershing II and cruise missile deployment, should still be ready to withdraw the new weapons. Now that deployments are under way, then, realistically, the best that can be expected is an agreement numerically reducing land-based, intermediate-range weapons in East and West—but not a reduction back to zero. The fact is that from the beginning Western politicians and military leaders opposed a complete waiver of the projected NATO modernization. They agreed to the zero solution only because they were convinced of its rejection by the Soviets.

Contrary to the fears of the peace movement, Pershing II is not a weapon suitable for a disarming first strike against Soviet missiles. It is, however, suited for missions against fixed targets of high strategic value, e.g., bridges, airports and command-control centers. With respect to these targets, timing is critical: attacks on them would have to be launched relatively early to be militarily effective. This would provide a military incentive for the early use of Pershing IIs against such targets and, under such circumstances, for NATO to resort to the first-use of nuclear weapons.

How necessary are the Pershings? The fact is that they are not needed for nuclear retaliation or for escalation in response to the first-use of nuclear weapons by the Soviet Union. And the employment of nuclear weapons against targets intended to be covered by the Pershing IIs is already provided for. As for those targets whose destruction depends on critical timing, it is highly desirable that they be targeted by conventional weapons. Indeed, NATO ought to renounce the first-use of nuclear weapons.

At a renewed round of the Geneva negotiations, or as a new initiative to bring the Soviets back to the negotiating table, the United States should offer to separate the Pershing IIs from the cruise missiles. At the time of the walk in the woods, the American government objected to the abandonment of the weapons mix of Pershing IIs and cruise missiles. The Reagan Administration should drop this objection. As a bargaining chip for negotiations, the Pershing II may have been a good option, but this is not the first time that bargaining chips have developed a life of their own. I believe the option of the Pershing IIs can be dropped.

Some politicians, however, maintain that because of their specific characteristics, Pershing IIs, unlike cruise missiles, constitute an appropriate counterweight to the SS-20s. Abandoning them would therefore be unreasonable as long as the Soviet Union possesses SS-20s. In fact, the expectations based on the technological features of Pershing IIs are as exaggerated as the fears advanced by the peace movement regarding these missiles.

From a military standpoint, NATO can do without the Pershing II. Whether the United States will now agree to forego deployments is much more a political than a military issue. The interests of the Federal Republic of Germany, rather than consideration for the Soviet Union, demand a positive reply to this question. Such a reply would, moreover, considerably increase the credibility of the United States with respect to arms control. How the Soviet Union would respond to the separation of Pershing IIs from cruise missiles is a matter to be determined in the course of negotiations.

The United States should, without delay, announce that it is willing to postpone any further scheduled deployment of new intermediate-range weapons if the Soviet Union agrees to reduce the number of its SS-20s. The greater the number of SS-20s the Soviet Union is willing to reduce, the longer the United States should be willing to postpone the beginning of the deployments.

Considering the fact that Andropov's proposal indicated Soviet willingness to reduce approximately 90 of its 250 SS-20s aimed at Western Europe, the West could propose that, for each month its further scheduled deployment of cruise missiles and Pershing IIs is postponed, the Soviet Union dismantle ten SS-20s. Thus nine more months could be gained for negotiations, just on the basis of the proposal already submitted by the Soviet Union. In this way, during negotiations, we could get closer to our aim of drastically reducing the number of SS-20s.

Such a proposal would cause neither side to lose face; neither side would have to abandon its fundamental negotiating position. If this interim solution were adopted, it could lead to a negotiated compromise providing for such a drastic reduction in Soviet SS-20 missiles that the deployment of new American intermediate-range weapons would be rendered superfluous. If this should fail, the United States would retain the option of continuing its scheduled deployments, while the U.S.S.R. would have the option of resuming the buildup of its SS-20s targeted on Western Europe.

This proposal does not hinge on unilateral concessions by the West. It can only be opposed by those who, whether for political or military reasons, are more interested in the deployment of new American intermediate-range weapons than in a drastic reduction in the number of Soviet intermediate-range missiles.

The Need for Western Consensus

NATO has thus far been unwilling to adjust its dual-track decision and its implementation to conditions that have changed considerably since 1979. In part, the reason is the fear that the unity achieved, with difficulty, in 1979 would shatter. But it is also, in part, the result of erroneous conclusions drawn from the controversy over the neutron warhead in 1977.

Consensus within NATO on fundamental questions of defense and disarmament is an important element of its capacity to act. Time and again governments and responsible opposition politicians in all NATO countries have rightly emphasized the positive significance of this consensus. This is why Helmut Schmidt repeatedly pointed out that the West, in addition to having an adequate defense capability, must also pursue a consistent policy of détente and disarmament. Schmidt's view remains as relevant as ever.

Whether the West should try to offset Soviet superiority in certain categories of nuclear weaponry (Western superiority in other categories was usually not mentioned), primarily through arms control negotiations or by rearming, was a subject of controversy in the United States during the 1980 election year. This dispute continued after President Reagan took office. Voices within his Administration even expressed doubt that any negotiations should be pursued. As a result, the Reagan Administration's credibility with respect to arms control policy has suffered. Along with the Soviet Union, the United States must bear its share of the responsibility for losing valuable time that might have been used to carry on negotiations. Meanwhile, arms buildups in both the East and the West progress unhindered.

By consenting to postpone further deployments if fruitful negotiation appears possible within the foreseeable future, the West can demonstrate the value it places on a satisfactory, negotiated agreement. Such a move would increase the West's credibility in arms control by fostering a political consensus over security policy among NATO members. NATO's determination to rearm, if need be, would not doubted because it decided to give itself more time for negotiations. In 1979 no automatic chain of events was set in motion that rendered subsequent political decisions by NATO superfluous. After all, since arms control negotiations in Geneva began only after considerable delay, and since allied will has now been demonstrated by the commencement of deployments on schedule as a matter of principle, NATO should be prepared to alter a deployment schedule that was established in late 1979.

It is much better to gain more time to try to reach a satisfactory, negotiated accord by altering a schedule set several years ago than to continue deployments in the face of opposition by large segments of the population, political parties, and various pressure groups. The domestic political polarization within NATO member-nations provoked by deployments would create a bad atmosphere in which to seek a new, broad consensus on future Alliance security and disarmament policies.

Politically it was a serious error of judgment for the NATO dual-track decision to provide for the deployment of Pershing IIs and cruise missiles in the Federal Republic while limiting deployments in other NATO nations only to cruise missiles. Chancellor Schmidt was right to insist, as far back as 1979, that the Federal Republic not be maneuvered into a unique position with respect to the deployment of intermediate-range nuclear weapons. Rejecting such "singularity" was the inevitable consequence of the Federal Republic's politically and geographically exposed position. This is why Chancellor Schmidt was adamant that at least one other non-nuclear member be prepared to accept the new U.S. nuclear weapons. But this "non-singularity" should have applied to Pershing IIs as well as to cruise missiles.

Integrated Negotiations

A Euro-strategic balance including land-based, intermediate-range weapons disassociated from the U.S.-Soviet strategic nuclear systems balance could stir fears among European NATO members of a U.S. decoupling from Europe. The substance of the START (Strategic Arms Reduction Talks) and INF negotiations are so closely interconnected that it was a mistake to have separate negotiations. Those negotiations should now be merged, as suggested in the freeze resolution of the U.S. House of Representatives. It should be noted that in doing so, consideration of the so-called third countries' nuclear systems would be facilitated.

As members of the North Atlantic Alliance, France and Great Britain are pledged to political and military solidarity in the event of an attack by the Warsaw Pact. Since they are European nations, their nuclear weapons, in one sense, are Euro-strategic weapons. But the French and British nuclear missiles are overwhelmingly deployed on submarines. Only France has some land-based missiles. Submarine-based missiles, however, have until now been classified as intercontinental, strategic weapons.

Compared to the total number of nuclear warheads possessed by the United States and the U.S.S.R., Great Britain and France possess a relatively small number of nuclear weapons. But if their submarine-launched weapons, by far the bulk of the French and British strategic force, were counted as intermediate-range weapons and, as Moscow demands, balanced off against the exclusively land-based SS-20s, the consequences would be serious: given the planned increase in nuclear warheads on French and British submarines, the U.S.S.R. could legitimately oppose deployment of U.S. intermediate-range weapons without having to agree to a drastic reduction of its SS-20s.

Soviet insistence on considering British and French systems in the framework of an overall nuclear balance between East and West is legitimate. The Soviet Union justifiably points out that it must include the threat emanating from the nuclear weapons of all NATO members in its calculations. If the West deems the consideration of these weapons systems in INF negotiations inappropriate, it should commit itself to consider them part of START.

There are important geographic and military asymmetries between NATO and the Warsaw Pact. Within NATO, North America and Western Europe are separated by the Atlantic. This geographic circumstance made it necessary to link the United States and Western Europe in order to meet the risks confronting them. The great number of American, British and French—compared to Soviet—submarine-based nuclear systems is a result of the military-strategic asymmetry between NATO and the Warsaw Pact. Notwithstanding the construction of a new generation of Soviet nuclear submarines, this military-strategic asymmetry will continue into the foreseeable future. Like the geographic asymmetry, it is also best dealt with in terms of arms control. An arms control agreement should consist of a combination of common upper ceilings and agreed ranges of freely mixed subceilings for intermediate systems. In addition to subceilings for land- and sea-based systems, a comprehensive agreement might include regional limitations.

If there should be integrated arms control negotiations on land- and sea-based nuclear weapons, NATO could again review whether, instead of deploying the planned land-based, intermediate-range weapons, it should not modernize the sea-based nuclear systems assigned to the Supreme Allied Commander in Europe and supplement or replace them with other sea-based systems. The arguments that tipped the scales in the High Level Group against sea-based systems in 1979 during the preparation of NATO's dual-track decision were politically unconvincing. Given the developments which have since taken place, those arguments are also no longer valid in the light of recent advances in weapons technology. The military purpose of nuclear long-range interdiction can now be taken over by sea-based systems.

Battlefield Nuclear Weapons

Shorter range, battlefield nuclear weapons are in a "gray area" which has not thus far been limited or reduced by agreements. Ending the arms race in this gray area through an East-West accord is militarily at least as important for the Federal Republic as reaching satisfactory agreements on intermediate-range weapons.

In his address to the IISS in London, Helmut Schmidt correctly pointed out that an arms control gap exists between the MBFR negotiations in Vienna and the agreements on strategic nuclear systems. It is in the Europeans' interest to limit and to reduce nuclear armaments in this gray area. This can be done step-by-step, provided the individual steps are interrelated by an overarching political concept of security and arms control. Currently, in my opinion, NATO does not have an overall approach capable of generating consensus on this.

Notwithstanding their short ranges, the SS-21, SS-22 and SS-23 nuclear systems can threaten the territory of the Federal Republic. The Lance missiles stationed at present in the Federal Republic are aimed at West Germany's Eastern neighbors, while the Pershing Is can reach Poland.

The planned deployment of Pershing IIs and cruise missiles would not add measurably to the existing threat to Poland, Czechoslovakia and East Germany, nor to the Warsaw Pact's leading power, the Soviet Union. In light of the existing threats represented by FROG, Scaleboard and Scud, the additional threat from the SS-20s is less menacing to the Federal Republic than, for instance, to Great Britain, Italy, Portugal and also France.

On the other hand, the SS-21, SS-22 and SS-23, which are modernizations of the FROG, Scaleboard and Scud, would continue to threaten the Federal Republic if the Soviet Union were to reduce its SS-20 potential or even forego it. Given the Soviet Union's strategic nuclear weapons potential on the one hand and its short-range nuclear potential on the other, the relevance of an agreement on intermediate-range nuclear systems for the Federal Republic, as for its Eastern neighbors, is significantly more political than military. Only in case of a drastic reduction or a complete Soviet abandonment of shorter range nuclear systems, would the explosive force of SS-20 missiles constitute a quantitatively relevant additional military threat to the Federal Republic's territory. For the Federal Republic of Germany, the reduction of Soviet short-range missiles is as desirable as the substantial reduction of SS-20 missiles. The negotiations on intermediate-range weapons should gradually be associated with future negotiations on shorter range nuclear weapons. From a long-term perspective, this would form a counterpart to the already acutely needed closer association of the INF with the START negotiations. Agreement at the INF negotiations on a moratorium on short-range nuclear systems would be a first positive step in this direction.

A Nuclear-Weapons Free Zone

NATO should unilaterally decide this year on a considerable reduction of the battlefield nuclear weapons stored in Europe. After all, according to the NATO doctrine of flexible response, all that the West needs is enough nuclear weapons to confront the Warsaw Pact with the threat that the conflict might escalate to the strategic level should the Pact launch an attack. Thus the internal logic of flexible response is contradicted by the deployment in Western Europe of so many battlefield nuclear weapons as to be sufficient in themselves to stop a possible Soviet advance. Since their use would in any event trigger nuclear escalation, battlefield and short-range nuclear weapons must be measured by the same standard as the controversial intermediate-range weapons: the question must be posed whether they increase the danger of regionalizing a conflict—thereby decoupling Western Europe from the United States—or whether they ensure the U.S. link to the risks confronting Western Europe.

Viewed in isolation, battlefield nuclear weapons and short-range systems certainly increase the danger of decoupling. Theoretically, it is conceivable that a devastating war could be fought in Central Europe with only conventional and short-range nuclear weapons without any greater risk of escalation.

From the perspective of deterrence, anti-demolition munitions and nuclear artillery contribute little to NATO's military capability. Given their short-range, they tend to deter their own use. With technological developments, conventional weapons can increasingly be used to force the U.S.S.R. to disperse its units. The number of NATO battlefield nuclear weapons stored in Central Europe should, therefore, be reduced unilaterally by well over 2,000.

The Palme Commission proposed a nuclear weapons-free zone extending approximately 150 kilometers in each direction from the border between NATO and the Warsaw Pact. Agreement on such a zone should be sought even if compliance with it, particularly at a time of rising tensions, would be difficult to control. To be sure, the establishment of such a zone does not alter the fundamental military-strategic balance in Europe. Still, the advantages by far outweigh the risks.

Putting into effect the Palme Commission's proposal would mean that no battlefield nuclear weapons would be positioned along the borders of the two alliance systems. This would reduce the likelihood that nuclear weapons would be used in a conflict close to the border. It would lessen the military relevance of theater nuclear weapons. It could halt the trend of developing new, smaller nuclear weapons and thus, indirectly foster agreement on a comprehensive nuclear test ban treaty. Moreover, this proposal reduces the risks of a nuclear war restricted to Central Europe.

NATO's dependence on the early use of nuclear weapons must be eliminated without increasing the temptation to resort to conventional warfare. The reduction in the number of nuclear weapons positioned in Europe and the creation of a nuclear weapons-free zone would not by themselves reduce the risk of conventional war. A lengthy war waged with modern conventional weapons would cause as much devastation along the border of NATO and the Warsaw Pact as a short war waged with theater nuclear weapons. To make conventional war less probable, the reduction in the number of nuclear weapons stored in Europe, and the downgrading of their military relevance, should be complemented by agreements on controlling conventional weapons.

Politically, priority ought to be given to arms control agreements and measures for military confidence-building. Taking the MBFR negotiations out of their present impasse by establishing phased reductions based on upper limits and consenting to reliable verification to permit such reductions would be especially desirable. Participants would need to agree on the respective data required to control the reduction. Negotiations aimed at achieving stability through an approximate conventional balance between NATO and the Warsaw Pact should then complement and expand the MBFR negotiations. The planned conference on disarmament in Europe starting in early 1984 could also contribute to militarily relevant confidence-building.

"Conventionalizing" NATO Strategy

A conventionalization of NATO's strategy should seek to achieve a defense posture adequate to deter a Warsaw Pact attack without having to rely on the threat of nuclear first-use. Both in the United States and in Europe, discussion of the possibility of nuclear wars and of the devastating effects of the use of nuclear weapons has resulted in a changed evaluation of the moral legitimacy and military utility of threatening the first-use of nuclear weapons. The loss of moral legitimacy and military utility is closely interrelated. The credibility of the Western retaliatory threat suffers if it is lacking in democratic consensus; and its acceptance in democratic societies becomes fragile if deterrence comes to be perceived as inappropriate to the external threat. Conventionalizing NATO strategy would be a positive step away from military thinking in terms of nuclear warfare. Though nuclear deterrence would not be abandoned, the distinction between using conventional and nuclear weapons would be made clear. In view of the moral crisis of legitimacy besetting the doctrine of nuclear deterrence, such an approach seems called for.

Recent years have witnessed developments in weapons technology that have considerably improved, both quantitatively and qualitatively, the possibilities for conventionlization. It ought to be borne in mind, though, that even with conventionalization, the primacy of politics and strategy over technology, not to mention the priority of arms control, must assert itself. The focus must be on the possibilities of developing a defensive strategy provided by technological advances in weaponry and not on adjusting strategy and politics to the new weapons. Not everything technologically feasible is necessary or even desirable. Obviously, because of financial constraints, the conversion from nuclear to conventional weapons can only be the result of a lengthy, gradual process.

An unequivocal judgment on the implications of conventionalization for deterrence strategy is impossible. There is no doctrine that simultaneously strengthens deterrence to prevent war and which, in the event of war, facilitates conflict termination and damage limitation. Nuclear weapons increase the damage wrought by wars, and thereby act as a deterrent, but they weaken the prospects for conflict termination and damage limitation. With conventional weapons, the reverse holds true. In the final analysis, the nuclear and conventional weapons components of a deterrence strategy must be determined in the context of a political evaluation of risks.

The risks involved in conventionalizing NATO strategy can at best be reduced by weapons technology but not completely removed. A conventionalization of NATO strategy entails different risks for Europe than for the United States. But the problem of risk evaluation and risk linkage among the partners in the Western Alliance is primarily a political and psychological question. Particular weapons technologies are at best capable of making a balanced distribution of risks between Europe and the United States more credible, but they can never guarantee it in terms of foreign policy.

Toward a "Security Partnership"

Mankind will have to live with its capacity for self-destruction. Notwithstanding all efforts at disarmament, the threat of mutually assured nuclear destruction will continue to be part of the reality of the East-West conflict well into the coming decade. It is politically possible and necessary to downgrade nuclear weapons gradually from their position as strategic deterrents and reduce them to the level necessary for minimal deterrence.

Preventing war by deterrence is an ambivalent and paradoxical concept. It involves too many risks to suffice for a lasting preservation of peace. In particular, democratic societies cannot, in the long run, consider legitimate the possibility of mankind's elimination as a precondition for the maintenance of peace. Citizens justifiably expect that the danger of deterrence failing be matched by political efforts to maintain peace. The strategy of deterrence is acceptable only as a transitional approach to less risky strategies for preserving peace.

The doctrine of deterrence seeks primarily to preserve peace through military capabilities that instill fear and horror in the potential opponent. The concept of a "security partnership" strives for growing cooperation with the potential opponent, without neglecting one's own interests, so as to solve security problems jointly if possible. Mutual deterrence is to be complemented and eventually replaced by mutual security. The United States and Canada should participate in a security partnership between East and West. The beginnings of such a partnership can be found in the CSCE process and the Vienna MBFR negotiations.

The preservation of peace cannot be accomplished by the methods of deterrence. Anyone wishing to remove the risks it entails must therefore gradually replace the system of deterrence. The concept of a security partnership aims at reducing mutual fear through cooperation and the reduction of mutual military threats.

Security policy, particularly with respect to decisions on nuclear weapons, will continue to stir public controversy over the coming years. A new political consensus on security policy can only grow out of a new overarching Western approach to its relations with the Soviet Union and Eastern Europe. The concept of détente in the 1970s, based on the Harmel Report of 1967, seems a suitable point of departure for the development of such a Western approach in the 1980s. Developments outside immediate East-West relations in countries of the Third World also have to be taken into account.

Compared to the 1960s, a larger measure of equal rights and codetermination for the European NATO partners relative to the United States is called for. More codetermination and a healthy, relaxed self-confidence vis-à-vis the United States and the administration in office could free many Europeans from their fluctuations between automatic accommodation to Washington and irrational criticism of the leading Western power. What institutional arrangements should be adopted to further codetermination, including decisions on shaping nuclear strategy and arms control policy more effectively than in the past, are urgent issues requiring attention in the period ahead.